PLOUGHS

Spring 1999 · Vo   D0483477

GUEST EDITOR
Mark Doty

EDITOR
Don Lee

POETRY EDITOR
David Daniel

ASSISTANT EDITOR
Gregg Rosenblum

ASSOCIATE FICTION EDITOR
Maryanne O'Hara

ASSOCIATE POETRY EDITOR
Susan Conley

FOUNDING EDITOR
DeWitt Henry

FOUNDING PUBLISHER
Peter O'Malley

PLOUGHSHARES, a journal of new writing, is guest-edited serially by prominent writers who explore different and personal visions, aesthetics, and literary circles. PLOUGHSHARES is published in April, August, and December at Emerson College, 100 Beacon Street, Boston, MA 02116-1596. Telephone: (617) 824-8753. Web address: www.emerson.edu/ploughshares.

EDITORIAL ASSISTANTS: Kris Fikkan and Kathleen Stolle. STAFF ASSISTANTS: Eson Kim and Tom Herd.

FICTION READERS: Nicole Hein, Kris Fikkan, Darla Bruno, Amy Shellenberger, Laurel Santini, Eson Kim, Joseph Connolly, Emily Doherty, Billie Lydia Porter, Karen Wise, Michael Rainho, Tammy Zambo, Elizabeth Pease, and Wendy Wunder. POETRY READERS: Brian Scales, Renee Rooks, Jennifer Thurber, Jessica Purdy, Tracy Gavel, Paul Berg, Aaron Smith, Michelle Ryan, January Gill, and Christopher Hennessy.

SUBSCRIPTIONS (ISSN 0048-4474): $21 for one year (3 issues), $40 for two years (6 issues); $24 a year for institutions. Add $5 a year for international.

UPCOMING: Fall 1999, a fiction issue edited by Charles Baxter, will appear in August 1999. Winter 1999–00, a fiction and poetry issue edited by Madison Smartt Bell & Elizabeth Spires, will appear in December 1999.

SUBMISSIONS: Reading period is from August 1 to March 31 (postmark dates). Please see page 204 for detailed submission policies.

Back-issue, classroom-adoption, and bulk orders may be placed directly through PLOUGHSHARES. Authorization to photocopy journal pieces may be granted by contacting PLOUGHSHARES for permission and paying a fee of 25¢ per page, per copy. Microfilms of back issues may be obtained from University Microfilms. PLOUGHSHARES is also available as CD-ROM and full-text products from EBSCO, H.W. Wilson, Information Access, and UMI. Indexed in M.L.A. Bibliography, American Humanities Index, Index of American Periodical Verse, Book Review Index. Self-index through Volume 6 available from the publisher; annual supplements appear in the fourth number of each subsequent volume. The views and opinions expressed in this journal are solely those of the authors. All rights for individual works revert to the authors upon publication.

PLOUGHSHARES receives support from the Lila Wallace–Reader's Digest Fund, the Lannan Foundation, the National Endowment for the Arts, and the Massachusetts Cultural Council.

Retail distribution by Bernhard DeBoer (Nutley, NJ), Ingram Periodicals (La Vergne, TN), and Koen Book Distributors (Moorestown, NJ). Printed in the U.S.A. on recycled paper by Edwards Brothers.

CONTENTS

Spring 1999

Cover painting: *Splice* by Richard Baker
Oil on canvas, 14″ x 11″, 1996
Courtesy of Joan T. Washburn Gallery

Introduction

It's a December afternoon in Houston, and I'm stuck in traffic on Westheimer, in a strip of shopping centers—an unrevealing detail, since Houston mostly *is* a strip of shopping centers, more retail opportunities stretched endlessly along these roads than you'd think even the fourth largest city in America could ever make use of. To drive through nearly any part of town is to encounter a repeated string of terms which together make up a kind of local vocabulary: NAILS, COMIDAS, CELLULAR, AUTOS, ESPRESSO, FUTONS, TACQUERIA, BIG 'N TALL, SUSHI, SHOES. (My friend Alan Hollinghurst, visiting from London, asked, "Is all of America so interested in *nails*?")

Some fifteen percent of the cars registered in America are registered in Harris County, which gives some idea of the automobile's primacy here; this is a drivers' place, developed over the last forty years or so on flat and swampy land an hour from the Gulf Coast. This urban world's designed—to the extent it *is* designed—for the convenience of the wheeled, and largely inaccessible by any other means. It's the only place I've ever lived where the homeless and the panhandlers actually work intersections by the freeways, standing out in the sun with handmade signs (HOMELESS, PREGNANT, NEED HELP PLEASE) and hoping that drivers stopped at intersections will roll down windows closed up tight to keep the air conditioning in, even this close to Christmas, and dole out their spare change.

I'm stopped this particular afternoon because a heavy orange piece of equipment is blocking the street, beeping and idling loudly. In its big metal claw is a peculiar-looking object, a roughly textured stalk about twenty feet long, held horizontally in the air. It takes me a moment to figure out what it is: a palm tree, trimmed at the top, almost rootless, about to be set into place in a row of matching trees along the edge of a particularly glamorous strip of shops. The cordon this new palm will join is already decorated for the holidays: their trunks are wrapped in little white lights, and illuminated stars jut out into the air a dozen feet above the ground: a long row of Stars of Bethlehem, as if every one pointed to the location of a commercial miracle.

This is the sort of juxtaposition which this city offers all the time, and in fact it's one of the things I really like about living here. I came to Texas a few months ago, for a new position in a wonderful creative writing program. I knew from my first week that I loved the job, and knew equally that this sprawling, unlikely town was going to take some serious getting used to. The skies were big and dramatic, full of towering clouds blown up from the tropics; the city was low-slung and, at first glance, truly disorderly. Houston's never had zoning laws, which means that an adult bookstore sits next to a "luxury townhouse loft complex," a car wash by a cathedral, a museum by a bodega, an "erotic cabaret" by a Radio Shack. What do you want to buy today? the town says. And if you want to build it, go ahead. This lack of restriction seems metaphor for a larger kind of de-centeredness. There's no real geographical center, no heart of things; a car culture makes everything a destination, nothing any more central than anything else. There is no dominant culture, and just barely a dominant language; in some areas the street and shop signs are in Spanish, in others Vietnamese. A teacher friend told me that there are some fifty-two languages in use here. In the classes my partner, Paul, is teaching, there are students named Gustavo, Batya, Senait, Jameka, Blas, Rogelio, Vonda, Mohammed, Chitra, and Bobbie Lee. Wildly disparate lives go on in the same city, entirely separate, occasionally overlapping. There are exclusive neighborhoods, of course, maintained by something called "deed restrictions," but even those are pierced by stacked freeways, and minutes away from collapsing apartment complexes side by side with new corporate towers poking up randomly here and there, all conjoined by the ubiquitous shopping centers: FAX, BUFFET, QUIK LUBE, CHRISTIAN BOOKS.

What surprised me about all this, after the initial shock a New Englander feels on entering the rawly energetic Sunbelt, is the odd exuberance of it, an unexpected feeling of human energy, the room, even in these endless asphalt acres, for individual expression. (What else are all those shops promising NAILS in big bright letters offering? Some sense of personal distinction, expressed as stripes and diamond chips, five-color lacquers, metallic two-tones.) And I began to understand that this is what the future looks like; if America has a ready example of life in the twenty-first century, this is probably it: artificial, polluted, a little dangerous, and completely confusing, yes—but also interestingly polyglot, open-ended, divergent, entirely unstuffy, and appealingly uncertain of itself. Which reminds me of a rather brilliant thing that Salman Rushdie said, in defense of his novel: "*The Satanic Verses* celebrates hybridity, impurity, intermingling, the transformation that comes of new and unexpected combinations of human beings, cultures, ideas, politics, movies, songs. It rejoices in mongrelization and fears the absolutism of the Pure. Mélange, hotchpotch, a bit of this and that is how newness enters the world."

This understanding—the bracing impurity of the future—still startles me a little. I'm a child of fifties and sixties sci-fi; the future had a whole design ethos, which was about streamlining, a perfection of ideal solutions, sleek arcs of plastic and metal. The futuristic was, in other words, modernity, in a kind of idealized, chilly form. But postmodernity shows us that the old predictions of what was to come—which was a sort of vision of the triumph of earlier avant-gardisms—isn't to be. And I suspect this is true in literature, too. Distrust, dear reader, whoever says that the future belongs to the non-narrative, or to New Formalism, or to minimalism, or even to the kind of formal self-consciousness and quick juxtapositions we've come to call "postmodern." Here in Houston, it looks like the future belongs to everything. And what I first took as disheartening disorder begins to reveal an interesting richness and variety of life between the cracks, along the seams; there's much more to see in Houston than first meets the poor eye overwhelmed by all this visual info on the horizon.

Rushdie's right; newness is "entering the world" in the form of various literary practices rubbing against each other, a cheerful polyglot disassembly of boundaries. An odd thing about literary history is how the breaking down of boundaries—consider the innovations of the Modernists, for instance—is so quickly followed by the work of flinging them back up again. It seems to be in the nature of avant-gardes to ossify; what begins in a spirit of adventure soon calcifies into codes. But if Houston at the end of the century is any indication, we may expect that experience is about to challenge whatever certainties about art we might arrive at; we might expect that growth, excitement, energy in poetry and in prose will come from collisions which won't let us hold our realms—either in terms of content or of form—apart.

That palm tree decked in its holiday finery, newly upright, looks both lovely and out of place; it's a stab at beauty and a sales-pitch come-on; it celebrates life in the heart of winter here where there isn't much winter. It reaches for the "natural" in an environment manipulated to the point where that term is an empty one. It is a gesture which plays on nostalgia, sure, but one so strange as to ultimately go beyond the cynical. Palm and star are far from home; maybe they represent the reinvention of tradition. Might this bright, tawdry new world display some loveliness, a strange kind of authenticity—its falseness complexified, if not exactly canceled out, by all these odd new conjunctions?

In that spirit, then, here is a collection of the polyglot, a slippery and contentious bunch of work from which it would be difficult to deduce, I think, a central aesthetic thread, a party line, a poetic policy. Well, okay, it isn't minimalist, it tends to believe that more *is* more. That experience, be it of the world or of the inner life, is worth representing, and that language is capable of such a task. It is work interested, in various ways, in the lived experience of social and political life, in the experience of being informed by externals (which are not, when it comes to culture and language, really outside us anyway). Otherwise, the doors are open, the possibilities large. Hooray for that. If it has a unity, then the common ground is—like Houston's—energy, vigor, a ferocity of encounter, a sense of freshness released by the unpredictable.

BOB HICOK

Once a Green Sky

A deer was on Linwood and I asked the forest
to come and retrieve her, curl its slow hammers
around our houses and decipher brick into scraps
of clay. My hardest wishes are for and against

ourselves, delicate locusts, ravenous flowers
with an appetite for even the breaths
between the spaces. Say you are alone. Pretend
everyone emulates you. Imagine if alone

the idea of the conversion van, the strong touch
of burrito wafting from the bodega, never
germinated in the cavernous brain. Hands
are no more clever than kneading dough,

the weapon of choice is sleep, the gods we adore
eat their own ribs, supplicant postures
of apology break out simultaneously in each
cabin and in exactly the same way. Impossible, okay,

move on. What if instead I owned one TV
and shared it with you on weekends, Lucille Ball
eating chocolate after chocolate as we laugh
in tribal reflex. If there was just one car

we touched the third Sunday of each month,
licked the leather seats, turned the engine
over and ran behind the bushes, terrified
at the growling dog we'd created, could this be

enough? There's a surprise in all flesh, this
is the purpose of eyes, to find and convey shock.
The deer and I faced as mistakes of context,
errors of intention, and she shot into the same

confusion one street over, we are saints
of replication, my house is your house, my
pierced navel your erection, the deer sniffed
for the green mist, thrashed through an archipelago

of false indicators, islands of shrubs that lasted
five paces, ten breaths, until she ran
into the mouth of a Saturn. From skulls I know
the architecture of her bones, lacy nostrils,

the torsion grooves of ligaments, just as kissing
a shoulder I have faith in the cup
and ball that work the joint, making it curl
into pleasure. I can't shrug gravity, the *Holy*

Spirit Force, but if possible would dream
silks of what contains us, the habit to make,
to adore the crystal chandelier
whose frail music each day is a dirge

for a hundred species. What if the forest
followed the deer, not into death but through
my living room, what if the rain ate my den
and you and I, unrolling a set of blueprints,

realized the sky is aspiration enough? Or if you
and I, reaching for a vowel, for the last
piece of coal on the stack, gave
silence, gave the eventual diamond back.

Chorus

Annual festival of the god of reborn souls and abandon,
The young drunken one who dies and in springtime rises:
From all over the City families come to the great amphitheater
Bringing picnics of roast fowl, rounds of bread, cheeses,
Preserved salt meats, clay jars of wine and citron water,
Feasting all afternoon on the stadium's grassy terraces
All in civic ease together, witnessing the terrible cadences
Of matricide, fratricide, betrayal, revenge, and defiant ambition.

And the show, while religious—the stage is the god's altar—
Takes place as a public competition: eminent citizens
Sponsor the dramas, paying the chorusmaster and writer,
The Chorus shouting and thrusting and retreating in unison,
Their gestures fluid, then stiff, then once again fluid, fully
Prescribed as in Yom Kippur, Ramadan or Easter ritual
But also Super Bowl, also high school tourney or rally
Local as much as divine, the ecstatic piety communal.

And since the tragedy makers the rich men commission
Vie for prizes awarded at the drunk god's festival
It also resembles Academy Awards, Emmys, Pulitzers,
All focused on the City arena—City of slavery, of oppression
Of women, willed by husbands who got them from fathers
As property to their own sons. Feel it at the revival,
Train station, ballgame: the breathing public organism.
And the chanting male chorus moves to a military rhythm:

A blind man who desired to join his countrymen in battle
Was able to fight, because he had learned the steps and gestures
Of the squad chanting with interlocking shields braced and flourished
And the heavy spears with their barbed bronze points, cruel,

Piercing and gouging in blind unison, the rhythm one creature's
Aggregate will, each unseeing trusting all to do their part
Thrusting and charging as one, keeping time though you perished
In the Chorus, martial, holy, carnival, carnal, the civic art.

LUCILLE CLIFTON

Jasper, Texas, 1998

i am a man's head hunched in the road.
i was chosen to speak by the members
of my body. the arm as it pulled away
pointed toward me, the hand opened once
and was gone.

why and why and why
should I call a white man brother?
who is the human in this place,
the thing that is dragged or the dragger?
what does my daughter say?

the sun is a blister overhead.
if i were alive i could not bear it.
the townsfolk sing we shall overcome
while hope drains slowly from my mouth
into the dirt which covers us all.
i am done with this dust. i am done.

ALICE FULTON

Maidenhead

In the closet the dress lives, a deep white in its vinyl
bag, eternal, the empire waist
so stylish before her time and after,
its crêpe ivoried, tartared like a tooth, feeding on
what leaks through
the zipper's fervent mesh, an unmentionable,
unworn, waiting,
immortally in mind. Open

a window, please, I'm feeling faint. On the bus home
from school, I'm reading Dickinson, living on her

aptitude for inwardness and godlessness, thinking
of the terror she could tell to none
that almost split her mind.
She made solitude honorable. But how hard
it would be to keep ink off a white dress
or keep black cake crumbs or lily pollen off,

how difficult to have only one dress and that one
white. Unlikely really, likely

to be a myth. But don't tell me that at seventeen.
I wear the same harsh uniform each day.
Narrow choices seem natural, strictures
more common than their opposite,
and I am always famished, crushed
on the bottom stair, the door closing
its rubber lips on my hair, trapping
lengths of it outside—

Last one in is an old maid. Your aunt is
mental, some kid says. There is a lace

of nerves, I've learned, a nest of lobe and limbic
tissue around the hippocampus, which on magnetic resonance
imaging resembles a negative of moth.
She felt a funeral in her brain. Somehow I get the fear
of living in the world's unlove forever
better than I get the cheerleaders' braced grins.
I understand my aunt's mind as the opposite of
Dickinson's, though Dickinson's also was unnormal, her white
matter more sparkingly aware.

You understand the dress in stanza one is mine,
my one white dress, in which I'll never

shine at graduation, in whose chaste V
the nuns won't stuff linty lumps of Kleenex
to keep covertness whole. In winter in upstate
New York, the snow is too bright on the bus window,
too crusted with singular crystals that toss
sun around inside them the way diamonds pitch
the light between their facets,

gloss to gloss. My aunt lived alone, as you do,
and if that sounds presumptuous, I meant it

in the sense that your head is mostly cloistered
though symptoms of your innerness leak out.
You know, the blush of a pink diamond
is caused by structural strain.
But her aloneness was deeper, I think,
than your own. Hers extended miles below
the surface, down, deep down
into pleats where no interfering rays
can reach and thought is not veiled

so much as sealed. A cap of lead.
Not veiled

since a veil's a mediatrix, at least in the West,
negotiating sun and glance. Veils screen
a virginal reserve = = the mind, I mean, or maidenhead,
a crimp at the threshold, figured as door ajar or slip
knot now, once thought to be homogeneous,
a membrane nervous and dispersed
throughout the body, more human than female,
both linkage and severance, the heart and brain
sheathed in its film of flesh and pearled
palladium effect. It is the year the nuns change

their habits at Catholic High, while the senior girls
spend recess studying *Modern Bride,* learning

how Honiton = = a bone lace
favored for Victorian veils = = was rolled
rather than folded for storage, sprinkled
with magnesia to remove the oily substance
which gathered after contact with the hair,
cleaned by being covered
with muslin and the muslin lathered
and rubbed until the lace below was soaked,
at which time it was rinsed, dried betwixt

the folds of a towel and sunned
for twelve hours till it looked new

and had no smell. If anything has no smell, it's a gem
and gems are seldom, the rare results
of deviance beneath earth's skin, of
fluky stresses that get carbon to exalt into
the flicker of a pre-engagement ring, a baby diamond
as solid and as spectral as
a long white dress flaunted by a
girl with nothing else. There's an optical effect,
interference, I think it's called, that puts the best

light on a gem's flaws, transshimmering
its fissures into vivid = = Your flaws
are the best part of you, Marianne Moore wrote,
the best of me, too, though as I write it, I recognize
an obvious misquote. Stet and stet again,

place dots under material marked for deletion
and let it stay, let the starved crystal raise

its hackles across the gap inside the gem = =
the trapped drop become a liquid memento,
let wave trains of light collide
from aberrations and give the thing a spooky glow.
Prove—like a Pearl. The paranormal glow

of "orient" of pearls exists between
the nacre shingles, and nacre begins, as is

well-known, with injury, a dirt that must be
slathered with the same emollient
used to line the inside of the shell. Solitude deepens,
quickening, whether hidden or exposed as those girls
sunbathing by the gym at noon in the thick of winter,

Janelle, the only black girl in the school,
who covers the white album with foil

and buries her face in the blinding book it makes
so that, as she explains, her skin might reach
the shiny jet of certain Niger tribes
or the saturated blue-black of subdural bleeding.
Her transistor, meanwhile, plays a blues that goes

I got a soundproof room, baby, all you got to say is
you'll be mine. I visited

Dickinson's white dress in Amherst where
it stands in her room, looking so alive it might be
spectral but for the missing head. The phantom pains,

escaping diagnosis, led to bolts of shock—
and tines of shudder—volting through
her mind, my aunt's, that is—stricken into

strange, her language out of scale to what
she must have felt, and Dickinson's metaphors—

And then a Plank in Reason broke—no help.
The doors are locked
to her little house, she has removed
the knobs, leaving deflorations you can peek through
once your eyes adjust. Up the stairs and to the left

beyond the thresholds' velvet ropes you'll glimpse
the shell-pink walls and hope chest full of failed

trousseau besides the single bed.
Look in upon that sunburst clock, the china creature
on a leash, some pearls unstrung, convulsions of—
the Frigidaire and oilcloth and radiator's
blistered pleats, the slot in which
we slip our fare—

"I sweat blood over this," the dressmaker sighs
at the final fitting, and I can believe it,

the pattern—imported, the seams—so deep,
the stitches—so uncatholic and so—
made for me. *Snap out of it*
someone says as we gain traction and wind
parts my hair, parts the comfort drops
my lenses float on, and I lean against
the door, the white lines vanishing
beneath us = = the measure rolling on the floor.

A Vigil, 2 a.m., County Jail

Waiting for their release—
for the shoes without laces,
the belts kept from suicide
—drumming, *When*
will they be released,
when and will they ever?
The hours so used
to their own sequence
cannot pass one another.
Diamond Ear waits here
for his *esposa,* and inside
the held-in selves stare
at their feet. They hate
the unbound, personal
tongues of their shoes.
Wives' eyes streetside
lynx on the transparent
jailhouse door. The stone
custodian entombs its men
in an infinite repeat of cells
like the guls in Persian rugs,
no escaping the eternal motifs,
the old, irresistible recurrences.
Will the stronghold
unbolt, will the men
spill out like rubble, gravel
at the foot of a weir,
will they sluice out, clean
and valuable again?

Then, in the darkest
hour out they pour,
their few clothes flying,

not birds migrating
into a pale limit of glass
but liquor wasting from
the crack in the punchbowl.
The women, too, tough flutter
of shirt, not wings,
day legs tossed onto
cold night. The lost,
the drowned, and the plagued,
paroled in a bunch,
not sorted like washing
and eggs and nails.
And they don't all look so hurt
but glad to be loose
in their own T-shirts
to drift toward the bank
of chilly telephones.
Only one or two
get an embrace.
And I am chewed
by the serrated beauty
of a street tree, its raggedy
light-bronzed royalty
pinned in cement,
in its firm house
stationed to stretch out
as big as its life meant.

In Her Image

French postcard, circa World War I

In agreeing to be the crucified woman,
she knew she would need to hang there
with no pockets, no purse, no pearls.
She would know how to stretch into it
when the time came. Did she enjoy
an innate ballerina who could express
befitting grace? While still her bearing
should look disciplinary, chastening.
Express duress. She must suffer
while blooming with a boast of pulchritude
the lighting director could work with.
At the tryouts, the rest of us were already
too mangled with practice nails, and slivers.

She stepped right up, and now she is *holding* on.
Jesus as evangelist from girlhood, a young savant
known for finespun sayings and secrecy
revealed as sorrow. Her death would fall
somewhere in her menstrual cycle.
Her belly invites most—soft and so
slightly split into those two lobes
which make apricots and peaches
superior to the moon. Lustrous,
a stage-curtain rope knots right over
pubic hair. Feet bound with ribbon,
a satin tether to appeal to some, she
ails ungaunt, her edges sled-round,
cambered. Coifed in the same style
as her carnality: in even waves, marcelled.

Are agony's good looks art's job,
or labor's contract, or sex's by swoon?
Whatever, they're hers. And the age's.
Real senselessness, stupefying power

over lives, eventually tore men's
faces off. Their leaders made millions
rot millions. Many choked on rats' mud.
Flies had no teeth for skulls
so there it stopped. What did this have to do
with our sacrificing, sacrificing our breasts
barely between a triangle of bleeding nails?
How we numbed evil. How unbearable
we made goodness feel.

Poem for the Breasts

Like other identical twins, they can be
better told apart in adulthood.
One is fast to wrinkle her brow,
her brain, her quick intelligence. The other
dreams inside a constellation,
freckles of Orion. They were born when I was thirteen,
they rose up, half out of my chest,
now they're forty, wise, generous.
I am inside them—in a way, under them,
or I carry them, I was alive so long without them.
I can't say I am them, though their feelings are almost
    my feelings,
as with someone one deeply loves. They seem,
to me, like a gift that I have to give.
That boys were said to worship their category of
being, almost starve for it,
did not escape me, and some young men
loved them the way one would want, oneself, to be loved.
All year, they have been calling to my husband,
singing to him, like a pair of soaking
sirens on a scaled rock.
They cannot believe he could leave them, it isn't
vanity, they themselves
were made of promise and so they believed his word.
Sometimes, now, I hold them a moment,
one in each hand, twin widows,
heavy with grief. They were a gift to me,
and then they were ours, like little nurslings
of excitement and plenty. And now it is summer
again, late summer, the very week
he moved out. Didn't he whisper to them
wait here for me one year? No.
He said, God be with you, God

by with you, God
by, for the rest
of this life and for the long nothing. And they do not
know language, they are waiting for him, my
Christ they are dumb, they do not even
know they are mortal—sweet, I guess,
refreshing to live with, beings without
the knowledge of death, creatures of ignorant suffering.

Hunters and Gatherers

Rick had been searching for the Pillings' address for over twenty minutes, and the hungrier he became, the harder it was to concentrate on the dimly lit street signs, the six-digit numbers stenciled on curbs. Westgate Village was a planned community an hour away from the downtown loft where Rick lived, and its street names were an endless rearrangement of the same bucolic phrase: Valley Vista Circle, Village Road, Valley View Court. Each one-story ranch house looked nearly the same except for the color of its garage door, and Rick, who'd skipped lunch, began to wonder if the entire suburb was a hunger-induced hallucination. Jerry Pilling, giddy as a kid at the prospect of throwing a party, had given Rick hasty directions over the phone so many weeks ago that Rick now had a hard time deciphering his own scrawl. He pulled over to the curb, squinted at what he'd written on a scrap of paper, and tried to retrace his turns. All the while, digestive juices sluiced through his stomach, and a dull ache came and went.

Rick was about to give up and head for a phone booth when a Mustang crept past, the driver peering this way and that, on the prowl for an address. Jerry had described the party as a chance for his wife, Meg, to meet a group of his gay friends, and after much wrangling she'd finally agreed, but only on the condition that she could invite her hairdresser, the one "avowed" homosexual she knew. Rick had a hunch that the man driving the Mustang was Mrs. Pilling's hairdresser—the skin of his face was shiny and taut, his silver hair moussed—and decided to follow him. "Avowed" had about it a quaint, anachronistic ring, and Rick pictured a dandy in an ascot, hand raised as he swore some sort of oath. Sure enough, the Mustang pulled up to the right address within minutes. A house with double doors and deep eaves, it sat at the end of a cul-de-sac. *Pilling* was chiseled on a wooden sign, the front lawn glowing greenly in the dusk.

Rick had met Jerry Pilling on a midnight flight from New York to Los Angeles. Returning home from his one-man show at a SoHo gallery, Rick was solvent and optimistic for the first time in a year. Seatmates in the back of the plane, the two of them struck up a conversation, or rather, Rick listened across the dark heartlands of America as tiny bottles of Smirnoffs accumulated on Jerry's tray table. "Meg and I are Mormons," Jerry told him, shaking the last drops of alcohol into his plastic tumbler, "so we aren't allowed to drink. But I bend the rules depending on the altitude." He touched Rick's arm, and his breath, as pungent as jet fuel, sterilized the air between them. "I'm terrified of flying." This was the first of Jerry's confessions; soon they came with escalating candor, the consonants softened by booze. "Do you know any Mormons?" asked Jerry. "Personally, I mean."

"Only impersonally," laughed Rick.

"Well, take it from me, not all of us are polygamists who bathe in our holy undergarments. There's lots of ways to be a Mormon; at least, that's the way *I* see it."

"There's a Mormon guy at my gym," ventured Rick, "who wears the garments under his workout clothes, even in summer."

"Or proselytize on our bicycles."

"I'm sorry?"

"Not all of us proselytize on our bicycles."

Rick pictured Jerry listing from a Schwinn.

"Listen," said Jerry, giving Rick a let's-lay-our-cards-on-the-tray-table look. "Are you by any chance...I don't mean to be presumptuous, so forgive me if I'm wrong, but you haven't said anything about a wife, and I was wondering if you're..."

"Gay?"

"I knew it!" blurted Jerry, slapping his armrest. "I have a sick sense—sixth sense—about these things. I am, too!"

To Rick's way of thinking, Jerry was unduly excited by this coincidence, as if he'd discovered they shared the same mother. Still, he found something ingenuous about the portly, balding stranger beside him. He eyed Jerry's wedding ring, and with no prompting whatsoever, Jerry launched into the story of his marriage. "I only recently told Meg that I fooled around with men in college. Groping a house-brother, that sort of thing." This piqued Rick's interest, and he had to steer Jerry back to the subject when, trying to recall the name of his fraternity, he was side-tracked into a muddled pronunciation of Greek letters. "The point," continued Jerry, "is that I wanted to write off my college flings as trial and error, youthful confusion. But after six children and twenty years of marriage, I couldn't ignore my thing for guys. College men especially. Studious types. Blond. With glasses." Jerry sighed. "The more I tried to pray it away, the stronger it got."

The plane hit a patch of turbulence over Kansas. Snug in his seat and buffered by vodka, Jerry didn't seem to notice. A few passengers shifted beneath their blankets. A baby bawled in the forward cabin. "We counseled with the church elders, Meg and me, and they thought that male companionship—strictly platonic, of course—would help me 'scratch the itch,' as they put it. So we decided to stay married and faithful, and I'm going to make some homosexual friends." Jerry brightened. "We'll have to have you over for dinner."

"The church *wants* you to have gay friends?"

"Hey," said Jerry, shifting in his seat. "They didn't say homosexual or not. But 'male companionship' is open to interpretation, don't you think?" He stirred his drink with an index finger, then sucked his finger and took a swig. "According to the church, if me and Meg get divorced, old Jerry here wanders around heaven for time immemorial, a soul without a family."

It was delicate: Rick didn't want to mock Jerry's religious beliefs, but he found this punishment cruel and unusual. Not to mention superstitious. "Do you really believe that's what would happen?"

"The idea scares me whether I believe in it or not. An outcast even after I'm dead. Lifelong bonds coming to nothing. Estranged from my very own kids." He chewed an ice cube and shivered. "I joined Affirmation, a group of gay Mormons, and they say the church is run by humans, and humans don't know everything there is to know about the Creator's plan; only one judgment matters in the end, and at least He'll know what made me tick and how I tried to do what's right. But Rick," said Jerry, leaning close, "here's where I part company with the folks at Affirmation: They're skeptical about a man staying married."

"You mean, about a gay man staying married?"

"Isn't that what I said? Anyway, living in a family makes me happy. My kids are turning into people I like, and the little ones shriek and swamp me every time I walk through the door. Chalk it up to my having been an only child, but even when they're fighting and crying, the chaos is kind of cozy, you know?"

"What about your wife?"

"I'd tried to tell her when we were dating, but she'd shush me and say the past didn't matter. It probably didn't occur to her I was messing with men. She wanted a husband, and I wanted to be normal; in that respect we were meant for each other. And here I am." Jerry looked around, then whispered, "I'm the only man Meg has ever slept with. And let me tell you something: I've never pretended. I've always loved her, and I always will. In the bedroom, too. Love must count for something, right?" The seat belt signs were turned off, and a low electronic bell rang throughout the cabin. "Sorry if I talked your ear off," said Jerry. "I should really keep my big mouth shut. But keeping quiet wears me out a lot more than talking." His head lolled toward the oval window. Rick leaned forward and gazed out, too. Beads of condensation gathered on the glass. Below them, as far as the eye could see, dawn tinted the rim of the earth; roads and rooftops and plowed fields—tiny hints of human habitation—were just becoming visible through thin, drifting layers of clouds.

The double doors swung open, and there stood Mrs. Pilling. Her tight auburn curls were a miracle of modern cosmetology, their true color and texture unguessable. She glanced back and forth between Rick and her hairdresser, smiling nervously. "Did you and Oscar come together?" she asked. Perhaps she assumed that Rick and Oscar had crossed paths in the small province of their "lifestyle." Rick felt a pang of sympathy for Meg. She's trying to hold up the walls, he thought, just like the rest of us. Dressed in slinky blue culottes, eyelids dusted with matching shadow, Meg appeared every inch the camera-ready hostess; the only thing missing, lamented Rick, was a platter of canapés. He felt certain her stylish outfit was meant to show her husband's unconventional friends that she was a woman with flair, not the stodgy, narrow-minded matron they might have expected.

"It's serendipity," Oscar told her, handing over a bouquet laced with baby's breath. "We met tonight on this very doorstep."

"Oscar treats me like a queen," said Meg, plunging her powdered nose into the flowers.

Jerry Pilling darted out the door. "Gentlemen," he bellowed, "welcome to the hinterlands!" His hail voice and vice-like handshake were far more manly than Rick remembered. Dressed in loose black linen, Oscar rippled as Jerry pumped his hand. "Meg's raved about you," he told Oscar. "Says you're the only man who can give her hair volume."

"Noblesse oblige," said Oscar. He turned toward Mrs. Pilling. "Meg, dear, you'd better get that nosegay into some water."

Rick and Oscar followed the Pillings into a spacious living room, as ornate, thought Rick, as a rococo salon. Overstuffed sofas and chairs were piled with tasseled pillows. Stripes and plaids and herringbones collided, vying for attention. One wall was an archive of framed family photographs. Jerry and Meg pointed to the pictures and boasted about their kids in unison—a long, overlapping roll call—and it sounded to Rick like they'd given birth to a happy hive, several more than the half-dozen children Jerry mentioned on the plane. Snapshots in which the whole family posed together had the voluminous look of class pictures. Rick imagined the Pillings' grocery cart loaded to the brim with potato chip bags, Cheerios boxes as big as luggage, six-packs of soda, gallons of milk. While the Pillings, as verbose as docents, led him along the wall, Rick searched every tabletop for a bowl of peanuts or a wedge of cheese, finding instead an endless array of ceramic animals, dried flowers, and colorful blown-glass clowns. The clowns looked as though they were molded out of hard candy, and Rick could almost taste their antic faces.

"Where *is* your brood?" asked Oscar.

"Simon's at debating. Mandy's at ballet. The rest of the kids have already eaten. They're in their rooms doing who knows what." Jerry nodded toward a hallway that burrowed deep into one wing of the house. Light seeped from beneath its row of doors.

"I'll check on the kids," said Meg.

"How 'bout I show you the grounds," said Jerry, slapping them both on the back.

The yard was a vast expanse of concrete with a kidney-shaped swimming pool in the center. Lit from within, the pool threw woozy refractions onto the surrounding cinder-block walls. Pool toys bobbed atop the water like flotsam from a shipwreck. An inflatable shark, bleached by the sun, floated belly-up. Jerry bent down at the edge of the pool and fiddled with the water filter, which made a shrill sucking noise; from behind, it looked as if he were trying to drink the pool through a straw. Blood sugar plummeting, Rick wondered if it would be impolite to ask for a Coke, or whether he should wait until something was offered. He scolded himself for being a recluse; if he got out of the studio more often, he might know how to behave in these situations.

The sliding glass doors rumbled open, and Meg ushered the remaining guests into the warm night. Mitchell Coply was Jerry's dentist. A man in his early forties, he had the slim, diminutive build of a schoolboy. A lock of hair sprang onto his forehead no matter how often he brushed it away. His puckish appearance was contradicted by tired, melancholy eyes behind his gold-rimmed glasses. During the round of introductions, Mitchell was soft-spoken and shy about eye contact, the kind of man incapable of concealing his sadness. Jan Kirby was an agent who worked with Jerry at a real estate office that specialized in new housing developments throughout the San Fernando Valley. Tall and broad-shouldered, Jan wore a pinstriped pants suit and running shoes. After meeting the other guests, she stood perilously close to the edge of the pool and faced the deep end, hands on her hips. Lit from below by the pool light, she looked to Rick like a deity about to part, or walk across, the water. "After dessert," she said in her husky voice, "let's go skinny-dipping." It took everyone a second to realize she was joking. Mrs. Pilling wagged a finger at Jan—naughty, naughty—and gave a fair imitation of laughter.

By the time the guests reassembled indoors to see the Pillings' remodeled kitchen, Rick was actively praying for snack food. The thought of salty pretzels possessed him, though he'd have happily settled for Triscuits, Cheese Nips, anything with weight and flavor. Meg Pilling ran her manicured hand across the width of a new refrigerator, like one of those models who stroke appliances on game shows. The built-in ice maker suddenly dumped a few chiming ice cubes into a tumbler. Mitchell nodded thoughtfully. Oscar applauded and said, "Brava!" Jan asked if the refrigerator could heel or play dead. Only after the demonstration did Rick notice the absence of cooking odors. The windows of the double-ovens were dark, the granite countertops barren. Copper pots hung above the electric range in descending size, mere decoration. Rick tried to fight his hangdog expression; hadn't Jerry said there'd be dinner?

"Folks," announced Jerry, after corralling everyone into the living room, "have a seat. The wife and I have a little surprise." The four guests squeezed among an avalanche of tasseled pillows and sank, side by side, into the plaid couch. "Honey," Jerry said to Meg, "you've got the floor."

Meg Pilling walked to the center of the room and faced the couch, hands clasped before her. She taught at Westgate Elementary, which explained her exemplary posture and the lilting, patient cadence of her voice. Rick had no trouble envisioning a troupe of mesmerized second-graders following her every order. He wondered if she was about to ask them to make their dinner out of paste and construction paper.

Meg cleared her throat and gazed into the upturned faces of her guests. "Jerry and I wanted to do something fun and unusual, so we've planned a really outlandish night." She grinned and shot a look at her husband. Jerry beamed back. "I bet you're all just itching to know what it is." As if on cue, everyone suddenly nodded and mumbled and shifted about. "Well...," she said, milking the suspense, "we're going to give you each five dollars and let you go to the store on your own—there are several excellent supermarkets in the area—so you can buy something to fix for a potluck!"

No one stirred or spoke. Rick wasn't sure he'd heard her correctly.

"We have all the cooking utensils you'll need," said Meg. "And that brand-new kitchen is just sitting there, waiting! The only rules are that you don't go over your five-dollar limit, and that you're back here within half an hour."

"Do we have to actually cook what we buy?" asked Mitchell. The idea of culinary effort seemed to depress him. "Can't we buy something frozen or from the deli section?"

Meg's smile wavered. Through the crack in her composure, Rick thought he glimpsed a hint of misery. "Now, that wouldn't be very creative, would it?" She looked at her husband as if to say, You've got to prod some people into the party spirit.

"I get it," rasped Jan. "Hunters and gatherers!"

"How primitive," said Oscar.

"I used to love scavenger hunts," said Mitchell. "Of course, those were the days when a kid could knock on a stranger's door without being molested or kidnapped." He pushed his glasses up the bridge of his nose.

"Well," said Meg, reviving her smile, "you're safe in Westgate."

"She's absolutely right," said Jerry. "If you're not back in half an hour, we'll file a report with the Bureau of Missing Persons." He removed a wallet from his back pocket and dealt out five-dollar bills. Peering up from a sitting position, reaching out for what amounted to his allowance, Rick had to admit that, fiscally speaking, Jerry fit the paternal role, confident and ceremonious as he handled money.

"Largess!" exclaimed Oscar. He took his five and winked at Rick.

"I ironed them," said Meg, to explain the crisp, unblemished bills. "Are there any more questions?"

Rick was going to ask the Pillings to give him explicit directions back to the house so he wouldn't get lost again, but he was nearly moved to tears by the thought that he could not only buy food for the potluck, but also something to eat right away, even before he got to the cash register. Rick was first to rise to his feet, a move which, considering the plush upholstery, took some leverage. The others straggled after him. Meg and Jerry each grabbed a knob of the double-doors and swung them open. "I wish I had a starting gun," said Jerry.

Mitchell paused in the doorway and asked, "Aren't you coming, too?"

From the way the Pillings looked at each other, it was clear this possibility hadn't crossed their minds. "We'll keep the home fires burning," said Jerry.

"Your best bet is to head back to the freeway exit," said Meg. "Toward the commercial district. You can't miss it." She watched her guests scatter across the front lawn, trudging toward their cars.

"Just look for signs of life," yelled Jerry.

Once inside his car, Rick noticed Jan in a Mercedes parked across the street, her face lit by the glow of a cigarette lighter, eyes rolling back as she took the first, languorous drag. Parked behind her, Mitchell furrowed his brow and squinted at a road map, disappearing within its folds. Oscar barreled by in his Mustang, shrugging at Rick and honking his horn. Jerry and Meg stood beside each other in the wide bright doorway of their sprawling home. They waved at Rick as he revved his engine, one fluttering arm per spouse.

Anyone who saw the Pillings in their doorway that night would have probably taken their happiness and compatibility for granted. Rick wondered what, if anything, Jan and Oscar and Mitchell knew about the couple's compromised marriage. He wouldn't have been surprised to learn that Meg and Jerry had let their secrets slip. It's easy, thought Rick, to confide in someone you see at work, or to someone who runs his fingers through your hair, or probes them into your open mouth.

As he pulled away from the curb, he couldn't help but marvel at the Pillings' elaborate domesticity: offspring, swimming pool, blown-glass clowns. While touring their home, Rick sensed that Meg and Jerry meant to impress each other more than their visitors: *See what we have. See what we've done. Our life together is no illusion, no mistake.*

Since Oscar seemed to know where he was going, Rick tried to catch up with the Mustang's taillights, but they shot away like comets near a street named Valley Court. Checking his rearview mirror for Mitchell and Jan, he saw nothing but the empty road behind him. Once again, Rick found himself navigating the maze of Westgate, its lawns trimmed, its houses all alike. He aimed his car toward a concentration of hazy light, a distant promise of people and commerce.

It had been so long since Rick cooked a meal, he was worried he'd forgotten how. Working in his studio till dinnertime, light-headed from paint fumes, he'd usually stand before the open refrigerator and nibble at scraps of food, or jump into his car and head for Casa Carnitas, the local taco stand. Dinners had been different when Eric was alive. The two of them sometimes dedicated entire nights to the alchemy of cooking; gas jets thumped when lit by a match, the raw becoming tender, the cold becoming hot. Chopping and stirring and sautéeing not only took time but seemed to prolong it, the minutes enriched with their arguments and gossip. When their studio grew warm and fragrant with the vapor of sauces, stews, and soups, Rick found himself believing that Eric might never succumb to the virus. Not if he could be tempted by food. Not if he gained weight.

"I wouldn't be so worried if I could put on a few pounds," Eric told him one night, peering down at himself as if over the edge of a cliff. The more elusive Eric's appetite became, the more time he and Rick spent planning and preparing meals. They began to visit ethnic groceries, farmer's markets, *carnicerías,* bakeries. At a restaurant-supply store near Chinatown, they bought a garlic press, a set of wire whisks, and what they decided was their most frivolous purchase to date: a lemon zester. Although he often couldn't finish a meal, Eric insisted that cooking gave him pleasure, distracted him from the neuropathy that numbed his lips and hands and feet. They had sex less often now that Eric was home all day, groggy from medication, and Rick suspected that their libido, rerouted, had given birth to lavish repasts.

In the early evenings, Rick cleaned his brushes, climbed the stairs to the sleeping loft, and crawled into bed beside Eric. The mattress lay on the floor, surrounded by issues of *Art in America,* bottles of AZT, and crumpled clothes. Rick would reach beneath Eric's sweatshirt and rub his back while they watched cooking shows on television, both of them soothed by the warmth and give of skin. On channel thirteen, Madeleine Duprey might fricassee a game hen or make a sumptuous ratatouille, rolling her *r*'s with such panache, they began to doubt she was really French. Next came Our Man Masami, a chef who dismembered vegetables with a glinting cleaver and, laughing a high, delirious laugh, tossed them into a hissing wok. At six o'clock, a pale and almost inaudible woman on a cable station cooked entrées on a wobbling hot plate, her ingredients spilling on her clothes or the floor. Such clumsiness belied her excitement; she closed her eyes when tasting the food, chewing fast, a happy rabbit. They took notes while they watched, salivating. They cheered and grumbled like football fans, shouting out comments like "Needs something crunchy!" or "Too much cumin!"

Over time, however, it was Rick who grew padded with fat, his trousers tight around the waist, while Eric, whittled by the blade of AIDS, could barely bring himself to eat; cheeks hollow, eyes indifferent, he'd prod the food with a fork.

Alarmed by Eric's weight loss, Dr. Santos started him on a regimen of Oxandrin tablets, steroid injections, and cans of a rich nutritional drink. His weight finally stabilized, but his already pale skin continued to grow translucent. Rick began to notice thin blue veins beneath Eric's temples, wrists, and groin, a glimpse into the tributaries, the secret depths of his lover's flesh. Still, Rick held on to the hope that he was only imagining Eric's fragility, making it into something more ominous than it really was. Until one Sunday at the farmer's market.

They were walking back to their car, both of them carrying bags of fresh food. Eric had been in good spirits that morning, eager for an outing. Enormous clouds raced overhead, their shadows strafing the city streets. Taking a shortcut, they turned down an alley, and a blustery wind funneled toward them. Eric's jacket blew open—the bright red lining flared for an instant, as disconcerting as the sight of blood—and he toppled backward, landing on his back. Apples and onions spilled from the bags, scattering among the trash and broken glass that littered the alley. Sprawled on the asphalt, Eric couldn't move his arm, and Rick knelt down to cradle his head. "Is this happening?" Eric asked. An eerie calm tempered Eric's voice, as if he'd observed, from far away, the fall of some frail, unlucky stranger.

In the emergency room, while Eric was being x-rayed, Rick told the attending physician that Eric must have tripped on a crack in the asphalt and lost his footing. But later, sitting alone in the waiting room, he couldn't stop repeating to himself, *A gust of wind knocked Eric over.*

AZT, it turned out, had made his bones brittle, and so Dr. Santos discontinued Eric's antivirals while his fractured arm had time to heal. This caused a sequence of illnesses that worsened Eric's weight loss. The most dire was an inability to absorb nutrients, a condition difficult to treat because the battery of sophisticated lab tests could find nothing wrong. Now and then he managed sips of broth, cubes of Jell-O, diluted juice, but nothing he ate or drank sustained him. Eric was eventually admitted to the hospital for observation and tethered to an IV unit. Rick offered to smuggle into the hospital the heavy, soporific dishes Eric had loved as a child: biscuits with gravy, chicken-fried steak, ice-box cake. But the foods he'd once loved revolted him now, and Rick's offer made him feel like a finicky child. "Honey," he told Rick, "it's better if you don't try to feed me." For days Rick sat by the bed while Eric faded in and out of sleep, his meals growing cold. Nurses swept through the room and changed the IV bag that dripped into Eric's arm, a clear solution that bypassed the tongue, his body unburdened by texture or taste.

Despite daily infusions and the few bites of food he forced himself to eat, Eric was dying of starvation. "AIDS-related wasting," Dr. Santos told Rick in the corridor, "remains one of our most difficult battles." The doctor spoke in a solicitous whisper, but Rick heard surrender ring through the ward, drowning out authority and hope. "Do you understand," asked Dr. Santos, "how wasting works?" Rick knew very well how wasting worked: lips papery, eyes puzzled, forehead hot, Eric retreated into the stillness and solitude of his body. No wish or prayer or entreaty could restore him. "What more," he asked the doctor, "do I need to know?"

Looming above the smaller shops and strip malls that surrounded it, the Westgate Safeway had the glaring, imperious presence of an oil refinery or a power plant. Rick parked his car at the far end of the lot. He'd given little thought to what he might fix for the potluck. On the drive here, struck by a fresh sense of Eric's absence, he'd had to remind himself that a year had passed since his death. Except for teaching two graduate seminars at a local art school, Rick had spent most of that year in his studio, working on paintings of slender, disconnected bones glowing against a black background. Now that the paintings were being shown in New York, Rick had accepted Jerry's invitation as part of a plan to end his isolation and revive his flagging social life. He didn't know anyone like Meg and Jerry, which accounted for the evening's strain, and also its sense of adventure. Tonight, anything sounded better than returning to an empty studio.

The second he stepped through the supermarket's automatic doors, Rick heard a tune he recognized but couldn't identify, its perky, repetitive rhythms urging him down the aisles. Wandering past shelves stocked with eye-catching cans and packages, Rick became one big, indiscriminate craving. Everything looked appetizing. In the Pet Food section, basted dog bones seemed like the perfect complement to a sharp Stilton or a salmon pâté. In

Household Cleaning Products, pastel kitchen sponges had the fanciful, minty appeal of petits fours. The linoleum throughout the store was creamy white and speckled like spumoni. "Your eyes are bigger than your stomach," he remembered his mother saying when he'd heaped his plate with more than he could eat. Once, he'd learned about the world by putting its pretty objects in his mouth—the dusty taste of a wooden block, a bitter, waxy bite of Crayola—and tonight he'd reclaimed, without even trying, this long-lost infant wisdom.

When he rounded the corner, he caught a glimpse of Jan, in her pinstriped suit, jogging toward Gourmet Foods. With his head turned, Rick almost ran into a man who was handing out samples of Inferno Chili. Standing behind a folding table, he wore a white apron and stirred a pot that was heated from beneath by Sterno. Peering inside the pot, Rick saw kidney beans, chunks of tomato, and bits of ruddy onion. The concoction bubbled like lava, small eruptions burping from its surface. "Try some?" asked the man. He held out a plastic spoon, a dollop of chili steaming at its tip, the smell robust and peppery.

Before Rick even began to chew, chili lit the wick of his tongue, his taste buds scorched by exhilarating flame. His eyes watered, nose ran. Perspiration beaded on his skin. He wrenched the spoon out of his mouth and grabbed a can of the stuff, as if reading the ingredients might explain the unearthly surge of heat. "A taste of hell in every bite!" exclaimed the devil on the label, grinning maliciously. Rick opened his mouth, half expecting to exhale fire and torch the store. The man in the apron handed him a tiny paper cup filled with Gatorade. "Only thing that cuts the burn," he said. "That cayenne's got a kick." When he smiled, wrinkles radiated from his brown eyes. His black mustache was waxed at the ends, his jaw shaped like a horseshoe. Rick wanted to thank him, but his throat had closed, leaving him speechless. "Here's one for the road," said the man, offering Rick another shot. At first, Rick wasn't sure if his gallant, folksy manners were real, or his languorous twang authentic. He studied the man through tearing eyes. His name tag read *Earl.* Dazed in the aftermath of chili, cool air wafting from the dairy case, Rick couldn't stop staring.

Ordinarily, Rick wasn't attracted to dark-haired men, or to men with mustaches, especially waxed. Any guy who reminded him of pot-bellied stoves and tooled-leather belts had always struck him as so remote from his own tastes and sympathies as to be practically extraterrestrial. In the past year, though, every man seemed alien to Rick because he didn't look or smell like Eric. He'd dated two men since Eric's death, but neither involvement lasted long. In the middle of an intimate dinner, he found himself staring across the table at masticating teeth, tufts of hair on the knuckles of a hand, and though he was glad his companions were mammals, these features were vividly physical without being the least erotic. The one time he did have sex, it was to prove to himself that he could excite someone besides Eric. While flailing naked, he'd inventory the way he and his new partner made love: *now he's plunging his tongue into my mouth, now I'm licking the inside of his thigh.* He might as well have brought a clipboard to bed. After sex was over, Rick knew he'd been a lousy lover, mired in the past, hopelessly distracted, as spontaneous as a windup toy. And now, at the Westgate Safeway, of all places, while Muzak tinkled in the glaring air, Rick's desire awoke from hibernation. Earl returned Rick's gaze—there was no mistaking—with the same flirtatious curiosity. "What brings you to the Safeway?" Earl asked as he slowly stirred the Inferno.

Coated with dust, its brown enamel faded by the sun, Earl's ancient station wagon looked like a boulder that had rolled into the parking lot. Rick carried the folding table and cooking equipment while Earl gripped a cardboard box filled with cans of Inferno. Now that Earl had taken off his apron, Rick could better see the outline of his body and the motion of his ropy limbs. Earl propped the boxes on the roof of the car and fished in his jean's pocket for keys. The Golden State Freeway roared in the distance. "By the way," said Earl, "you can keep your five bucks; there's no finer way to promote a product than feeding it directly to the people."

"It isn't my money," Rick reminded him. "And besides, Inferno will be the bargain of the party." They lifted the tailgate, loaded the car. As they slid inside and slammed their doors, the station wagon creaked on its springs. "Just throw that crap in the back," said Earl. "I wasn't expecting company." Rick reached down and chucked cans of Sterno, a box of plastic spoons, and a stack of paper cups into the back seat. Crumpled McDonald's bags and a few empty soft drink cans littered the floor. Rick told Earl that the station wagon reminded him of his studio when he was too steeped in work to think about cleaning, to give order to anything but art; the disarray was industrious. "I guess I can see that," said Earl, nodding at the compliment and idling the engine. "It's in me to give a thing my all. Before selling Inferno, I did a stint at a pitiful little radio station in Buford. My spot was called 'The Classical Half Hour,' but it was more like a fancy fifteen minutes. I'll tell you, though, this gig's as solitary as being a DJ. During long hauls, I've been known to interrogate myself just to have a conversation." Earl laughed and shook his head. "The things you'll confess, alone on the road." He twisted a knob on the dashboard and a tape deck sputtered to life. "Johann Sebastian Bach," said Earl, upping the volume. "Best antidote I know to a day of Muzak." He threw the station wagon into reverse.

"Do you know your way around Westgate?" asked Rick.

"All I know these days are supermarkets. Anyplace in between is just gas stations and motels. If it doesn't have a checkout stand, it's not on my map. Don't you know where we're headed?"

The directions were locked in Rick's car back at the lot, and after convincing Earl to keep him company, he wasn't about to suggest they turn around. Rick peered through the bird-droppings and insect remains that splattered the windshield, doing his best to guess the way back to Meg and Jerry's. He couldn't help but interpret the windshield as a good omen: Earl had traveled numberless gritty miles to meet him, and even if they only spent one night together, the unlikelihood of their having met, combined with the tape deck's welling arpeggios, made their impromptu date seem predestined. "It's funny," said Earl, "to have a passenger." As Rick leaned toward the dash and squinted at street signs, he told Earl about his conversation with Jerry on the plane. All the while, he could sense Earl staring. Lack of subtlety was one of Earl's most appealing traits, and Rick had to use every ounce of restraint and concentration to keep his mind on the road. But when Earl rested his hand on Rick's thigh, impulse ordered Rick to pounce. He dove head-first into the driver's seat, yanked Earl's shirt from his jeans, and kissed his stomach, the flesh warm, taut, and salty. Earl gasped and arched his back, allowing Rick to lift his shirt higher. Rick pulled his head back far enough to see Earl's stomach in the emerald light of the dashboard. Wind from the open windows ruffled Rick's hair and blew into his shirt. The velocity of the car, the rumble of the engine, the bumps in the road felt metabolic. "That," he said, peering up from Earl's lap, "is one beautiful bellybutton." Rick couldn't help but notice that the things he said and did that night were unlike him, or at least unlike the recluse he'd become, and his audacity, like a file baked in a cake, freed him from the cell of himself. He circled and probed Earl's navel with his tongue.

"Yikes," heaved Earl. "You *are* an artist!" He steered the car to the side of the road with one hand and gripped a hank of Rick's hair with the other, pressing him against his stomach. The station wagon grazed the curb and lurched to a stop, its cargo rolling and clattering in the back.

Earl's mouth was wet and generous, his hard jaw covered with stubble. When he moaned, his bony chest rattled with pleasure, an erection tenting his jeans. The more they kissed, the more Rick realized how alone he'd been, and the more alone he realized he'd been, the deeper and greedier his kisses became. The restless pressure of Earl's hands had the power to cause and alleviate need. Finally, the two of them pulled apart long enough to catch their breath and make a plan: an appearance at the potluck, back to the Safeway for condoms and Rick's car, then on to Earl's motel.

After ringing the doorbell, the two of them waited on the front stoop, cooking equipment in tow. As Rick reached out to squeeze Earl's shoulder, he remembered reaching beneath Eric's sweatshirt and rubbing the supple muscles of his back. The memory, blunt and unbidden, lingered in his hands.

When no one answered the door, they snuck inside the house as quietly as thieves. In the living room, Earl's eyes widened. "Wow," he whispered, appraising the place. "Beats the rooms at Best Western." The guests had gathered in the dining room, where sliding glass doors opened onto the backyard and the luminous pool. Everyone stood around the table and added to the hum of conversation. Even from a distance, Rick could hear the strain of people trying to keep the ball of small talk aloft. A surprised hush greeted Rick as he walked into the room with a stranger. Oscar looked at them quizzically. Rick introduced Earl all around, counting on the possibility that the Pillings were too bent on being "outlandish," and too restrained by good manners, to object to an uninvited guest. Earl dipped his head and repeated each name. "I sure appreciate the invitation," he said to Meg. There had been no invitation, of course, but Earl's gratitude disarmed Mrs. Pilling and prompted her to chime, "We're glad you could come."

Meg had set the table in anticipation of a buffet. The white tablecloth matched the napkins fanned atop it. Empty china bowls and plates waited to be filled with food. The crystal chandelier cast a faceted light. Rick had to admit that Earl made a scruffy addition to the pristine room and the well-dressed guests; as a result of their feverish making out, his hair was mussed, his mustache frayed. A stew pot dangled from the end of his arm, and he stood there with the dreamy, limp demeanor of a kid who'd just awoken from a nap. Rick didn't dare imagine what *he* looked like, though he suspected a hickey was imprinted on his neck. Propped against Rick's chest was a cardboard box. He set it on the table and explained that, for a mere five dollars, Earl was going to treat them to an up-and-coming American meal.

"Up-and-coming, indeed," repeated Oscar, who could skew any phrase toward innuendo.

Rick shot Oscar a warning glance.

Earl cleared his throat, straightened up, and mustered all the salesmanship he had left. "This is just about the most savory pot of chili you'll ever taste," he said, in his polished, disk-jockey modulations. "Inferno's aiming for a three-year growth plan with a product-recognition goal along the lines of, say, your Dinty Moore or Del Monte." He lit a fire beneath the pot and began stacking cans of Inferno into a pyramid, display-style. "We've got quite a few backers in South Dallas, the kind of ranchers who're all wallet and no cows."

Mitchell smiled for the first time that night, and Rick was sure he found Earl attractive. Jerry saw Mitchell smiling at Earl, and his body tensed. It occurred to Rick that Jerry might harbor a secret crush; didn't Mitchell possess the collegiate look, glasses and all, that had made the airborne Jerry rhapsodic? Noticing the devil on the cans, Meg folded her arms and turned to share a look of consternation with her husband. When Meg saw Jerry staring at his dentist, the same hunch that occurred to Rick seemed to cross her mind. Her arms slipped loose and fell to her sides.

This was the aspect of parties that Rick found most wondrous and suffocating: one suddenly became entangled in the invisible lines of lust or envy or resentment that stretched between the guests, a web of intrigue whose threads are so elusive they only exist in the realm of speculation. Suddenly, Rick was walloped by an idea: a diagram of the party would be his next painting. He imagined, stretching across a wash of muddy color, filaments of strong, unspoken feeling.

Once Earl had completed his pitch, the others took turns presenting their purchases. Jan dredged from a Safeway bag, one by one, a can of baby corn cobs, a tin of Norwegian sardines, and a glass jar crammed with tiny white cocktail onions that, even beneath the flattering light of the chandelier, looked haplessly subterranean. She placed the offerings on the table. Everyone eyed the foreign labels. "It's gor-may," she enunciated. "I once had a girlfriend who lived for pickled foods." Meg blushed, as if "pickled foods" were a euphemism. Jerry began to struggle with the jar of onions, huffing and gritting his teeth until Jan grabbed it from his hand and twisted off the lid with a flick of her wrist. "You loosened it for me," she told him, and Rick imagined that she'd had to say that, or something equally reassuring, to many men in order to downplay her prowess and spare them embarrassment. She dumped the onions into a bowl.

Mitchell contributed three boxes of Munchables, a packaged assortment of lunch meats, crackers, and processed cheese spreads that could be served in various combinations. He ripped open the boxes and, shoulders hunched in an occupational posture, prepared a plate of meticulous hors d'oeuvres.

Oscar proffered a one-pound box of marzipan from Heidi's Kandy Kitchen, a concession he'd found tucked away in a strip mall. Everyone o-o-ohed at the replicas of plump strawberries, ripe bananas, and sanguine apples. Each fruit exuded an oily sheen, a sweet almond odor. Meg said, "They're precious," and gingerly nibbled a miniature orange. What happened next was something that Rick, who considered himself visually sophisticated, if not downright jaded, had never conceived of, let alone seen.

Meg let loose a warble of horror, and her right eyelid began to widen and contract, the eyeball rolling languidly in its socket. Her otherwise mild and maternal presence gave way to a kind of lascivious rapture, and if Meg weren't mortified into silence, Rick would have expected her to purr with delight, lick her own shoulder, or nip at the air. The instant Jerry became aware that his wife was seized by a fit of involuntary blinking, he pulled out a chair into which Meg plummeted. With one hand she applied pressure to her tremulous brow, and with the other held her eyelid closed by the lashes. While trying without success to control the upper half of her face, her jaw went lax and revealed a nasty mash of marzipan. When Meg realized she was flashing food at her stunned guests, she shut her mouth with such force, her teeth snapped like the clasp of a purse.

"Oh my God," yelped Mitchell. "I read about it in dental school, but I've never seen it happen firsthand!"

"What is it?" barked Jan. She stood erect and ready, as though prepared to pin Mrs. Pilling to the floor if the spasms worsened.

Meg waved her hand as if to say, *Don't look at me, please.* Everyone crowded closer.

Rick tried not to gape, but from this vantage point he could see Mrs. Pilling's pupil dilating and contracting in an effort to adjust to the changing light, an ocular phenomenon whose helplessness he found hypnotic. The body is such a mystery, he thought; you forget that your eyes are apertures, that your skin is a huge and vulnerable organ, that your muscles have a will of their own.

Mitchell cut through the huddled crowd and bent over Meg. "Is it Marcus Gunn Reflex?" he asked.

Meg nodded.

"You've heard of it?" marveled Jerry. "I'm very impressed." He dashed through the swinging door and retrieved a glass of water from the kitchen. While Meg took a couple of grateful gulps, Jerry rested his hands on her shoulders, his wedding band catching the light. "It hasn't happened in years, has it, darling?"

Meg poked and kneaded her own cheek as if putting the finishing touches on a clay bust. "I think it's stopped," she said. She tilted her face toward the light, eager for confirmation. Motionless and circumspect, the party gazed at Mrs. Pilling and waited to see if the twitching returned. A warm breeze blew through the screen doors. A swing set clanked in the backyard. Crickets throbbed on the lawns of Westgate. At last, Mitchell pronounced the episode over, and there came a collective murmur of relief.

"Marcus Gunn Reflex is rare," explained Mitchell. "It's caused when the chewing muscles and salivary glands are connected to the muscles that control the eyes. Anything can set it off: certain kinds of food, emotional stress, even Novocaine injected into the wrong spot."

"It's painless," said Meg, "but unpredictable and terribly embarrassing."

"And congenital," added Jerry. "Her mother first noticed it when she was nursing Meg in the hospital. 'It made my baby look like a little sucking glutton,' she used to tell me. 'So blissful at the teat.'"

Meg twisted around and glared at Jerry. "Thank you," she said. She took a deep breath and hoisted herself out of the chair. "Will you all excuse me." Meg fled into the kitchen, indignant and liquid in her blue silk culottes. Jerry hurried after her. No sooner had the swinging door stilled then there arose the angry clank of pots, a furious blast of tap water. The Pillings must not have been familiar with the acoustics of their new kitchen because all that decoy noise did little to mask their voices. "I'm embarrassed enough as it is, Jerry, without you regaling your friends with stories about my breast-feeding. They don't have to know everything about me."

"What do you mean, 'embarrassed enough as it is'?"

"I can't look at those people without thinking about what they do with each other in bed."

Oscar sighed a breathy, facetious sigh. "One look at me, and people think of sex."

"They don't do anything with each other," said Jerry. "They didn't even know each other until tonight."

Jan peeled the lid from the tin of sardines, releasing a briny reek. A regiment of fish stared back, darkly iridescent. "What are these marinated in, anyway?" she asked. "Motor oil?"

Earl surveyed the buffet. "This," he said, "is one cockamamie potluck." He hummed under his breath and dished chili into the bowls.

"Luck is the operative word in potluck," mused Oscar. "On the groaning board before you, what looks like mere food is actually the manifestation of chance." He waved a hand over the table. "Things come together in ways you'd never expect."

"And fall apart in ways you'd never expect," added Mitchell.

"Then don't think about what they do in bed, Meg."

"I can't be around them and *not* think about it. That's the problem with homosexuals."

"But this party was your idea as much as mine."

"No, Jerry. It was *your* idea. I agreed to this party because, after consulting with the elders, I was ready to do whatever it took to live up to our vows, to keep you happy and faithful. But you know what I found out tonight, Jerry? I found out I'm old-fashioned. And I'm tired of being polite. Men laying with men, women with women: it's a sin, period. And you condone it." Silverware clanked like scrap metal. "I saw you looking at that Mitchell."

Mitchell took a bite of chili, and his eyes began to water. "Even if I were attracted to Jerry," he said, "I'd never date a patient. Especially not a heterosexual. It's hard enough to find someone compatible; why would I want to make the odds impossible by going after a straight man? Besides, abscesses and gum recession don't exactly fan the flames of lust." He sniffed, removed a handkerchief from his back pocket, and blew his nose. "This is delicious," he said to Earl.

"Jerry was cruising the pants off you," said Oscar. "The man could use a few lessons in the art of the clandestine glance. Especially if he plans to stay married." He plucked a tiny pineapple from the table, turning it this way and that to admire its diamonded rind. "Meg is a lovely woman when she's not besieged by queers."

"Besieged?" said Rick. "I seem to recall being invited."

"In Texas," said Earl, "the married ones go to another town when they want to fool around. They'll do everything with another man but kiss him on the lips, and they think that makes them—"

"Pure as the driven snow," said Oscar. "It's amazing, all the intimate things you can do with another human being and still remain a virgin." As soon as he popped the marzipan into his mouth, he seemed, for a split second, tangible yet absent, lost in the confection's density and sweetness.

"Don't tell me you weren't ogling him," said Meg. "I have eyes."

"That's an understatement," said Oscar.

Jan fished a baby corn cob from a bowl. "Hold on, you guys. I don't blame her for being upset. It's another case of the wife getting the short end of the stick. I'm awfully fond of Jerry, but, at the office, he's one of the boys when he's with gay men and one of the men when he's with straight women." She poked the cob—a pale, extraneous finger—into the air for emphasis. "Jerry wants it both ways," she continued, "which would be harmless, I guess, unless you were married to him and had a horde of kids to take care of. None of us would want to be in Meg's position."

"Of course not," said Rick, "But the way Jerry explained it..."

Meg hissed, "You twist things around till they suit you."

"I'm trying to do what's best for—"

"Me and the kids? Spare me the piety, Jerry."

"For all of us, I was going to say. Don't second-guess me. So I think a man is handsome, what's that have to do with how I feel about you?"

"Nothing," said Meg. "And it hurts."

"I know what Jerry's going through," said Mitchell. "My ex-wife is still furious because I told her I was gay. And because I didn't tell her sooner."

"In other words," said Rick, "she's mad at you for failing at the marriage *and* for trying to make it work."

A glass broke in the kitchen. "Look what you made me do," shrilled Meg.

Mitchell gazed into his plate. "Do you think we should leave?"

"Not me," said Rick. "I don't care if they start throwing knives. I've waited all night to eat, and I'm not going anywhere until I'm full." He loaded his bowl, took Earl by the hand, and walked outside. At the pool's edge, Rick yanked off his shoes and socks, rolled up his pants, and dangled his legs in the tepid water. Earl sat behind him, knees against Rick's back. The two of them gazed into the night sky hovering weightlessly above the suburbs. "Sure would be nice to stay in one place for a while," lamented Earl. "Tomorrow I've got a gig at a Market Basket in Placerville." The bass notes of his voice vibrated in Rick's rib cage, like the rumble of a truck passing in the distance. Rick might have felt a pang of sadness about Earl's leaving, but the temperate air, the plentiful stars, and the pool as bright and fathomless as daylight fortified him against despair. Compared to losing Eric, he thought, all my future losses are bound to be bearable. But the moment he heard Earl speak again, he knew this wasn't true. "I wish I lived here," said Earl. His words were so plaintive, so burdened with yearning, that Rick laughed when Earl added, "But then I'd probably be in the kitchen scrapping with my wife."

Oscar and Mitchell and Jan walked toward the pool, a talkative trio. Each of them held a china plate filled with incongruous food. Rick recognized in their speech and gestures small flourishes of goodwill—a stray touch, a teasing retort—that a stranger might mistake for flirtation. When Jan delivered the punchline of a joke—"And the priest says, 'Young lady, when you get to heaven, Saint Finger is going to wag his Peter at you'"—laughter displaced the silence of the night. Somehow a party had sprouted in the Pillings' backyard like a dandelion through a crack in the sidewalk. Rick leaned against Earl's knees, eating and swinging his legs until waves slapped at the sides of the pool, sending rafts and lifesavers drifting on choppy, turquoise currents.

The sound of churning water drew two of the Pillings' children from their rooms. They materialized from behind the swing set at the far end of the house. The youngest, a barefoot girl in an oversized T-shirt—Rick guessed her to be about ten—sauntered toward the strangers. She plunked herself down by the water and tried to garner, without seeming to, as much attention as possible. When the inflatable shark drifted toward her, she flung out a leg and kicked it in the snout. The shark wheezed and sailed away. "I'm Yvonne," she announced.

"That's not her real name," said the boy from the opposite side of the pool, hands thrust in his pockets. Rick had no trouble imagining him as a grown man who inhabited the periphery of parties, lobbing skeptical remarks into the crowd, eyes animated by the same watchfulness that shone in them tonight.

"I'm the governess," announced the girl.

"She's my little sister," said the boy. "She likes to act bratty and pretend she's things she's not."

The girl went on, undaunted. "Are you friends of Mr. and Mrs. Pilling?"

The guests paused, considering her question.

"Excuse us," came the voices of Meg and Jerry from inside the dining room. Everyone turned to face them. Jerry stared forlornly into the backyard, as if he were outside the house looking in. "I'm afraid its late," he said, pointing to his watch. Meg said, "We hate to be party poopers." Their voices, strained through the wire mesh of the screen doors, were timid and thin.

Oscar bent over and lifted Rick, then Earl, to their feet. Rick brushed off his jeans and glanced at Earl with such overt, erotic promise, Oscar clicked his tongue.

Jan and Mitchell hurried their conversation, determined to fit in a few remarks before parting. "I bet your ex-wife will be more forgiving when she finds another husband," said Jan. "If I knew more heterosexual men, I'd set her up on a blind date." Mitchell agreed that things would be easier once she was coupled, but behind the gold-rimmed glasses, his eyes conveyed their native doubt.

The little girl and her brother bolted across the concrete, flung open the screen doors, and ran into the dining room. Yvonne nearly collided with her father, embracing his leg, and Rick wondered what it would be like to be grabbed by your brash and affectionate child just when love seemed the most farfetched. The boy gravitated toward his mother but remained aloof. He peered into the yard, waiting to see what would happen next. Ever the considerate hostess, Meg reached over and flicked a wall switch; an outdoor light suddenly blazed beneath the eaves, a magnet drawing moths from the night, their shadows churning against the house.

"Shall we take our leave?" asked Oscar. And the visitors headed inside.

Rick received a postcard from Arizona that depicted a jackelope, the imaginary offspring of an antelope and a jackrabbit. A postcard from Florida showed a freight train's flatcar loaded with an orange the size of a house. Earl sent the most surreal cards he could find, either because he favored them or thought they'd appeal to the artist in Rick. They arrived every few weeks, a reminder that the world's oddities were inexhaustible.

Eventually, however, the cards stopped coming, as Rick knew they would. He often chided himself for not writing back, but Earl never asked for a reply or included a return address. Besides, Rick was at work on a new painting, and, apart from a nagging set of technical and aesthetic preoccupations, he had little to talk about. He'd come to think of his encounter with Earl as a thing completed, an improvised composition that one more brush stroke would ruin.

And then, just as Rick was about to relegate his evening in Westgate to the past, a letter arrived from Meg and Jerry. It was one of those Xeroxed family newsletters sent out at Christmas. Rick thought of them as artifacts from his parents' generation, a form of braggadocio in the guise of a greeting, its gossip purged of secrets and upheavals. The Pillings' newsletter was printed on red paper decorated with sprigs of holly—Meg's choice, Rick was certain. Itemized in alphabetical order were the academic and athletic victories of their six children. Rick noted with amusement that nowhere was there mention of a girl named Yvonne. Other than parental hyperbole, the highlights of Meg and Jerry's year were reserved for the last two sentences: *We visited the big island of Hawaii in September, where we glimpsed the fury of a live volcano. Upon our return, Jerry assumed a position on the church's high council.*

Rick turned the letter over, searching for a salutation scrawled in the margins, or for some note that would say what became of Jerry and whether his equivocations persisted. But the margins were empty, and even the signatures were photocopied. Rick slid the Pillings' letter into the rolltop desk he'd inherited from Eric, and swiveled around to face his latest painting. The cavernous studio contained a homey commotion of paintbrushes, dropcloths, and old coffee cans encrusted with acrylics. Outside the windows, sunlight burned through the clouds and ignited random patches of the city—a glass high-rise, a peeling billboard—then quickly faded away. The fluid, moody light animated his painting. Its imagery was based on his recollection of the Saturday morning cartoons in which trails of enticing odor wafted from hot pies, freshly baked bread, and juicy pot roasts; then as now, he loved how those long ghostly arms rippled through a room and caressed a face, burrowed into nostrils, and beckoned to the hungry with curling fingers. Follow. Taste. Be sated. Rick leaned forward. Thanks to hours spent feathering wet paint with a small brush, tendrils of scent reached across the canvas. One moment they seemed to float closer. The next they seemed to recede.

Safe

What I knew was that part of my body
was leaving. A pinch of it on the flow
out through a bare arm surrendered
to the fluorescent scrutiny the clinic.
Like a bite, I was told, this tearing into,
and yet I did not look, did not care to see
the thickening in the vial, the silver stem
out of my skin. I lay on the examination table,
thinking: no harm— *A little,* she said,
the nurse in her dense perfume and whites.
I need only a little, as I admitted
so discrete an entry, as I, as I—

*

He was like the man with the glove
in that painting by Titian. I saw only
the brighter parts of him. Hands. Skin
in the open wedge of his shirt. He was
waiting for anyone, devotedly—for me tonight,
as I stepped into his throng of urinals.
One hand, like a scrap of paper, floated toward me.
The other rummaged for a zipper. Skin for skin.
I thought: I should ask. I should ask
for what I desire, as I knelt before him.
Yes, said his faceless voice, said as his hands
settled my head like a breeze persisting, said.

*

When the sin you have committed
is made known to you, you shall bring a goat
without blemish as your offering. You shall
lay your hand on the head of the offering,
and the offering shall be slaughtered.
The priest shall take some of its blood with his finger
and put it on the horns, and he shall pour out

the rest of its blood at the base of the altar.
He shall remove all its fat and turn it into smoke
on the altar for a pleasing odor to the Lord.
Thus the priest shall make atonement
on your behalf, and you shall be forgiven.

*

The gnawing on my arm took what it wanted,
which was no more than a sip. I said,
It's warm, I said, warm like the warm
of those nights when I drove to the park,
eased in among the parked cars, and waited.
One man led me across the cropped grass
to where night was darker, and then, in safety,
kissed me. I closed my eyes. I thought:
Blindly they wandered through the streets,
so defiled with blood that no one was able
to touch their garments (Lamentations).
I tugged at his shirt. It submitted. I lifted it off.

*

My head against the stall of the urinal.
Myself in the shelter of his body.
Stench smeared into the air and wet dark
of the tile floor. *To be merged, that is,*
into an utter oneness... I held on
as if trying to contain his breathing.
As if breathing could be contained.
I heard companions, felt a hand at my wrist—
the nurse as she read my heart's racing.
I need only a little, said as she loosened
the tourniquet, the outflow a scorch of a sudden.
(*The soul is a sort of fire or hot substance...*)

*

Can you draw out Leviathan with a fishhook?
Can you put a rope in its nose, or pierce its jaw
with a hook? Will it make supplications to you?
Will it speak soft words to you?
Will it make a covenant with you
to be taken as your servant forever?
Can you fill its skin with harpoons,

or its head with fishing spears?
Were not even the gods overwhelmed
at the sight of it? Who can stand before it?
Who can confront it and be safe?
Under the whole heaven, who?

*

So he led me across the cropped grass
to where night was our only protection.
We laid down in it, and he kissed me.
He said: *I'm safe,* he said, *I'm safe,*
as he lowered himself and kissed me.
I leaned back. I became an arch for his arms
to pass under. Later, gathering our clothes,
I watched him: so this is your face, stranger.
And I thought, Would it be you all along?
Were those your clues of grass I picked
out of my hair, you in my headlights
like a lesion on the dark?

*

Here, she said, *let me put a Band-Aid there,*
then peeled off her gloves, trashed them.
See, she said, *I needed only a little.*
As soon as she finished she gave me
a folder full of papers: *I hereby authorize the—*
An explanation of the— I understand that the—
Because to save himself there is nothing
a man withholds. *Just reach out your hand;*
just touch his bones, his flesh, and see—
that vial on the table: dark of those nights,
blood of those nights, skin for that skin.
I rolled down my sleeves. I buttoned them.

from Paragraphs from a Daybook

My life ago, in this renascent slum
shabby Jews in sweatshops, with irregular
papers, wherever they came from,
gathered mid-morning around a samovar
enthroned amidst rows of Singer sewing machines.
They trusted the Republic. They were last seen
being beaten with rifle butts onto sealed trains.
Their great-nephews are Orthodox extremists;
their great-nieces are hash-smoking anarchists.
Some of the sweatshops are high-priced oak-beamed flats,
but I live in one of their tenements
with smeared hallways, corroded pipes, centenarian drains
and five flights of ancient, patinaed spiral stairs
getting junk mail from clothes-jobbers and bureaucrats,
sheltered from fascists and the elements.

When I've described my life like this, I've lied
I also live in six airy rooms on upper Broadway
just south of Harlem, which I bought when my mother died
—a schoolteacher whose penury
left me the wherewithal for bedroom windows
with a view, two long blocks west, of the Hudson.
One friend thinks I'm a coddled American
hypocrite after she spent ten days with me there—
America, whose deep thumbprint of blood's on
cachectic brows from the Bronx to Zaire.
Addicts with AIDS warehoused in SROs
hidden on side streets south of Riverside
Drive might not find Sarajevo
or Kigali on a map, but tonight, they know
people like them will starve and freeze somewhere.

—which is Saturday night, so that's where my lover
is giving out condoms and clean syringes
door to door, floor to floor. Someone's had fever
for a week. She's shown an abscessed sore. Nobody scrounges
quarters or cigarettes.
                              Some rooms are neat.
Their tenants ask her in. There's a hot plate,
a kettle, pictures of cats from a magazine
taped to a wall. She sits on the chenille
bedspread, and hears about the son, fourteen,
who lives with his grandmother outside Asheville.
There are some rooms she'd rather not go in.
                                                    Her
colleagues, two medical students and a nurse,
each with a backpack and a sharps container
come down the stairs from the upper floors.
                                        Of course
she knocks on those doors, and goes in, when she's asked in.

At nine or so, she's done, and there's a table
set, amber liquid threading ice,
a cork drawn, bread broken, companionable
alto spirals, pulsed by the bass;
on the street, slang and sirens of upper Manhattan.
Robert is dead, and Melissa, and Geraldine,
Larry, Angel. Doris started Crixivan.
So did Wilhelmina. They're both in wheelchairs.
The grainy blowup on a gallery
wall—a man slumped onto a leatherette
sofa, eyes open, pupils rolled back: dead
is snapshot legacy or prophesy.
The smart-ass golden boy photographer,
Kevin, who started the needle exchange from his van
died in his living room of an overdose.

*   *   *

His ex, Eddy, will smoke up what's left to steal.
José is dead, of PCP pneumonia:
third bout, three weeks in hospital.

They both lived in the Hotel California,
a sixties ballad title, not at all
like the sixties, except in its surreal
aspect; cocaine and heroin
also something in common.
Every dry day, José sold used books
from a table on Broadway.
While a couple, they had house plants, six cats, cooked
arroz con pollo on a hot plate; José
fixed up found bicycles he carried in:
transient objects which will drift away
into the next binge of his next-of-kin

Daily she traverses the frontiers
health/sickness, sheltered/outcast, life/death:
doorways on dingy corridors,
sentences with pits dug underneath
them, the eloquence of absence or
presence (in from the street to wait for her).
Home, tired, she calls her friend,
gets the machine. The phone rings, and
it's not a patient with his viral load
and T-cell count come back
from the lab. Her friend is dead
at forty, of a heart attack.
Minutes ago, on tape, the alto voice
solicited her message with a joke
Dinner tomorrow night? Or brunch? Your choice...

An almost-empty Air France afternoon
flight to New York
(booked the same morning in the rue Caron
travel agency) carried me back
like a rich cousin, for a long weekend.
I thought about how frequently a plane
returned me to somebody's bed,
evoking desire instead
of the body as locus of loss.
Caresses once reminded me

of touching that palpable mass
in my breast, touching mortality.
Though now I count back years away from that
there's still a dismal kind of irony
that I'm here on this last-minute flight.

The heavy presence of so much raw grief;
the oddness of my being there in June;
the way she worked at it inside herself
the way a dog worries an open wound:
the ruined skin open, the thick pelt stiff
with blood, not knowing why it tastes like this.
I'd say, I'd salve, but I'm useless
in her corporeal distress.
I can't make this a normal Friday night:
a film, a meal, although she goes
along with it. We saw a movie, ate
as couples on Columbus Avenue
still stopped, at half-past-ten, to window-shop
the Birkenstocks and Kenneth Cole dress-shoes,
the sherbet-colored T-shirts at The Gap

*　　*　　*

Two funerals in June, in two
countries, in one week.
Death has a tendency to overdo
and life to border on the bathetic
In Paris, nobody that I know
is dying. The days unwind, a slow
ribbon toward midsummer. It rains
intermittently. No trains
or planes scheduled, I put my things in order.
New passport-stampings marks
the week of my, Ellen's and Zenka's border-
crossings, theirs into the final dark.
My mind flings itself toward tranquillity:
the Chinese girls turn cartwheels in the park
on the rain-lush *pelouse autorisée*

Refinishing the Hardwood Floors

from "The Changing Face of AIDS"

The day he came to give his estimate,
the rap he played came echoing amidst
the tall Victorians that line our street—
a jarring rumble, even in the cave
that they create. He wore a rumpled shirt
emblazoned with his name. "I'm Rafael—
it's nice to meet you, Dex." My hand seemed small
on shaking his, whose palm was etched and carved
with lines—it felt like corrugated steel.
We knew that he was ill; to do our part,
we try to offer jobs through special deals
for those in the community with AIDS.

He paused as we ascended, out of breath.
I wondered whether he was up to it:
our loft is huge, and traps the heat beneath
the skylights we put in last year. Besides—
the flecks of sawdust on the skeletal
black arms that braced him on the banister
were mixed with track marks, tiny dots of scars
along his veins. A loud dog barked outside,
which cued us to resume our climb. What changed,
so that I saw him shuffle down the hall,
delivered at its end to the airy stage,
cathedral-ceilinged, windowpanes so great

that in their frame his slender silhouette
seemed insignificant? He jotted down
some notes, unnerving me the longer that
he stayed. The room was getting hot, transformed
from what was heavenly beside the man
I loved (I felt the rush of it anew,

the thrill of making household plans with you),
to an approaching hell with Dex. His firm
touch interrupted me just then: inscribed
in shaky handwriting were figures penned
with, evident in their completeness, pride.
He told me he could start next week. At dawn

on the appointed day, he came with two
assistants. k. d. lang or Europop—
I wondered which CD would better do
to drown their racket out. Too frequently,
perhaps, I checked on them, my concentration
shot even worse by a recurrent thought:
a stranger in the house you and I bought.
The sanding led to toxic fumes; for three
long days we aired our new room's shiny floors
impatient to set foot in our creation.
I paid in cash, then rushed Dex out the door;
I felt so clean I cried, and couldn't stop.

MICHAEL J. CARTER

Billy Asked

Two months after she died, Billy asked:
How's Lynda doing?

Billy, I said, *she died, remember?*
Under the weight of supper's
constellation, the table wavered.

Manic, he'd cook and then he'd
insist on cleaning up: *it calms me.*

Just now remembering, I remember,
embarrassed, he's dead, too.

What's the distance between a source
and its shimmer? (A sink full of dishes,
a different wobbly table.) Billy,
frantic and kind, how are you?

July 3rd

Overcast till 4 p.m. Gunshot-like crackling
punctuates the hazy afternoon—
premature fireworks as neighborhood kids
prepare earsplitting festivities
in honor of Independence Day.
Bees big as doorknobs buzz drunkenly by,
barely able to remain airborne.
The dog races ahead through Elysian
Park. We're on a dirt trail that winds
through California scrub—scorched hillsides
of orange nasturtiums,
morning glories colonizing small trees,
trunks unreadably graffitied in blue.
Blooming yellow anise, pepper trees
and parched jade plants. Scrolled
white jimson flowers jut up, ready
to unfurl like small Torahs and reveal
their stern laws: *eat me at your peril*
heedless vision seeker, hungry infidel.
My beloved short-legged dog has something
suspicious between her teeth. I can tell
by the way she's holding it I'm going
to have to take it away from her—
it's some kind of contraband. She's thrilled
with her discovery, wants to eat whatever
it is right away. I have to tell her *drop*
that four or five times in a fake stern voice
before she obeys. It's a rodent torso—
a baby gopher or ground squirrel
from the waist up, tiny front limbs
all drawn in at the elbows, and the delicate
claws resemble a wren's. Its straight, yellow
buck teeth form the perfect gardening tool,

extending past the end of its whiskered chin.
The poor half-gopher's all dried out
by our desert weather. And I'm being mean
to deny the dog her treat, her fur-covered
meat prune. I tell myself I'm worried
about what the gopher died of—maybe
it'd make the dog sick, though most likely
the rodent's life ended from being chewed
in two, rather than some imagined
mammal plague I fret could harm my hound.
She regards me for a moment with tolerant
disdain, then trots off to sniff a beetle.
Black as a bobby pin, its shellacked butt
for some reason (mating stance?
insect religion?) thrust up in the air.

I follow the dog, convinced
of her superior wisdom. She paws
a puckered patch of mud,
almost tromps on a woolly caterpillar.
Another firecracker whistles and booms.
She'll take on rattlesnakes or pit bulls
without hesitation but really fears
these explosions. Last Fourth of July,
skyrocket noises got her so riled
she chewed the wooden blinds
to splinters and gnawed off part
of a table leg. When I returned
from barbecuing, I found her
crammed under my desk, shivering.
Normally, she's so stoic. A book
I've read only parts of says that
in Greece, around 300 B.C., the Stoics
believed nothing could happen
which was not part of nature's
perfection. Man's duty was to
cheerfully accept whatever occurred,
secure in the knowledge it was all
for the best. If you traveled to Egypt

and a Nile crocodile bit your first-
born in twain, or the oracle at Delphi
prophesied ruin for you and your issue,
or your daughter got leprosy, or your son
was enslaved and made to wait upon foreign
heads of state naked, or your wife ran off
with five illiterate monks you'd paid
to stomp your grapes into wine, you were
supposed to remain calm, unmoved by good
fortune or bad, beyond hope or fear.

After you died, little brother, people
offered condolences. Since you're with me
now every second, you accompany the dog
and me on this hike. Sometimes, to be kind,
friends gently suggested that since you'd been
so ill, maybe it was better you'd passed into
infinity, where out-of-the-body adventures
commence. Maybe it was for the best, they said:
you'd graduated to ash and thus your sufferings
had ended. I admire those Stoics, truly I do:
their attempt to relish every strange fate
the earth serves up; their faith in nature—
that seizure-prone, sexy, bloodthirsty girl.
I comb the dog's fur with my fingers,
picking out foxtails. I find a clod of dirt
sprouting nine kinds of grass and give it a kick.
When a lifetime finishes, proteins fold
themselves into useful shapes, like clothes
neatly stored in drawers for future use.
Then the devout, clannish Stoics
clap their nonexistent hands, and the applause
is just deafening. *Bravo,* they yell, jumping
up and down. They pound the red velvet arms
of their chairs, wad up their programs and pelt
the stage with them. *More, more, more,* they chant,
faces hot, eyes brimming. *Let us hurtle through
the world again. We demand an encore.*

Otus Asio

Number 280 in the Audubon Society Field Guide

At first it seems the most subtle
   of spirits, inhabiting invisibly this dense,
adumbral light at the bottom of the woodland
    understory, the rise and fall

of its own recurring phrase
   so tremulous, so mournful a tone, we resist
our impulse to pause beneath the trees,
    to pass our hands

in blessing over our hearts—
   and though it comes to us bidden, awing
out of the wavering green, the sort
    of fabled creature

once the familiar of myth
   and bewitchment, when it finally sways
above us, horned and docile on the arm
    of the maple, repeating

our imitative call,
   we see it's clearly the mottled little dukelet,
the lone scritch, the whickering owl
    in its gray phase, bird

of the most common public
   exotic, who follows us even as we follow it
deeper into the woods, the temporal world
    of moth and worm,

root and earth, of the wanton
   and wild, into the darkness, that place
to which we convince ourselves
     we've each returned.

A Little Beer During Fence Repair

Thank God for the beaver pond. You know
   I had my doubts about cutting the two-hour trail
      so close to the pond, but those animals

are not shy, and let me tell you: it was destiny.
   Those two men I guided last night? They said
      they had come all the way to Alaska

to fulfill an important task. They needed
   a beautiful place, with water. So? The pond!
      We arrived. I tied the horses.

The men went ahead, beyond the trees.
   Just as I finished uncinching,
      I knew what their task was.

The last girth dangled, dark and warm,
   close to its shadow on the loam, and it hit me:
      They are scattering ashes. I knew.

I stayed away, to give them their
   space. I watched the girth sway.
      And here's what's stayed with me,

all day: This man's body, his whole life,
   has come to this end, here, in this pond,
      with these men and the horses and me.

I was there for the termination.
   Can you understand what this means?
      It was the way an entire horse,

the whole animal, spills from the
    arc of a horseshoe to the hole of a nostril,
        the way the *flowing biology* must end

in space, must navigate uncertain
    boundaries with ground and air—privacy
        must mean even less for the dead—

but I did not look when the ashes
    were blowing, even though I knew
        when they were released, exactly,

and I won't go back to see them,
    though some may still be there,
        on the bank.

The Gift

We saw it on the side of the road,
its back legs splayed
like scissors that have come unhinged:
a rabbit dragging its ruined parts,
insisting on the sweet grass beyond the curb.
We knew it was dying, Susan and I.
We said *We should leave it,*
as we stopped down the road
and asked for a box
and came back with the brown, corrugated thing:
an offering of safety
or help in forgetting the green field.
After we had brought it to the fire station
where the fireman offered to beat it with a shovel,
we watched its breath become heavy and slow
until the eye went out and we were gone.
Then driving down the road,
at a restaurant, or waving through the street
in the summer wash of tourists, Susan would say
Dead bunny
and we'd laugh and laugh:
our secret code for our brokenness,
our persistent need.

Lessons in Another Language

In the summer of 1967, Nathan Bogmore never woke up before eleven o'clock. He was fourteen years old, and he slept with more intensity than he did anything else. Having just left the warm, rumpled mattress in the empty back room of their cottage, he stood at the front door in his pajamas, squinting into the day, wishing he could simply get back under the sheets and forget everything.

He heard his father moving around in the temporary studio he had made in the garage, and in the direction of the main house, down the road a quarter mile, there was the sound of drumming as the dancers did their warm-ups on the lawn. His mother was painting in her studio at the smaller cottage. His sister, a girl two years his junior who was named Genevieve Bogmore on her birth certificate, but called Jimmy by family and friends, was either dancing with the troupe on the enormous lawn at the main house or helping Mack water the trees that had just been planted on the edge of his property.

So much creativity going on around him only made it harder for Nathan to resist the urge to give up and go back to bed. It took a powerful effort to bust into the day at that late hour, and he wasn't sure he wanted to go to all the trouble. He looked down at his feet. Then he looked out into the woods directly across from the porch and saw a bunch of trees. What saved him, what saved him every time, was hunger. So he turned around, let the screen door slam shut behind him, and went into the kitchen to find some breakfast.

The school year had gone badly for Nathan, and even though it was summer vacation, he should have been up hours earlier studying his French. He'd managed to pass math and English, but he had failed French. To go on to the second level, he had to take summer school. The session ran for eight weeks in July and August, which meant that the Bogmores' peripatetic tendency would have to be reduced to weekend trips. All of that was discussed and resolved after the letter had arrived from the principal. No wanderings through New England, no week-long stays at the Jersey shore. Because of Nathan, they were going to have to endure the whole stretch of summer vacation right there in humid Philadelphia.

It was finalized. The box on the letter was checked, and Nathan was enrolled in French camp at Temple University. He would get there on his own, take the bus to the Broad Street subway and the subway to the Temple stop. He would not pay attention to the smell of urine in the underground tunnel or the trash whipping along the dusty street in the hot wind. He would simply go to class and then come home. It would be a long and boring summer, but in Nathan's mind it was a just punishment for his reckless disregard of requirements. The penance pleased him. It matched in its dullness the level of excitement he had felt at the start of the year when a slick and dangerous confidence had lifted him above the stupid entanglements of his classes.

But. And in the Bogmore family, the *but* was everything. Nothing was secure against the *but*. It could wedge into any resolution and blow it apart.

The *but* in this case was Phyllis. She invited the entire family to stay in the cottage on Mack's summer place in Connecticut. There was a studio in a smaller cottage for Judy, Nathan's mother, to paint in, and a very suitable garage space where Paul, Nathan's father, could have a kiln and a potter's wheel. All in exchange for a few hours every morning helping Mack plant some trees.

Judy had been delighted. She told Phyllis they would love to do it, and she'd call back the next day with a definite answer. That evening at dinner she related the proposal to the rest of the family. Already saved from a summer of hell, his mother was as giddy as a little girl. It made Nathan particularly joyful to know that he was going to be the one to destroy her plans.

"I failed French, remember? Summer school?"

"Nathan, don't be sarcastic," his father said.

"Oh shit," his mother said. "I had forgotten. You're sure you failed French? The grades aren't in yet, are they? Maybe you managed to squeak through."

Nathan went to the desk and pulled out the letter the principal had mailed to them the week before. "It says it right here. I failed."

His mother was ladling soup into bowls. That was the period of the one-pot meals. So she could have a longer day in the studio, she cooked chicken, beans, and vegetables on the weekend and made soup from it all week long, varying the ingredients so it wouldn't get boring. By the end of the week, everything was so mushy she just threw it all into the blender and Friday's soup was a brown purée. You could still find bits of carrot and chicken, which Nathan took the trouble to do because he liked food to be distinct.

"Wouldn't it be wonderful if Mack and Phyllis had a place in France?" his mother asked. "Then it would solve everything. You're having trouble because you don't know what the language sounds like. What you need is to be surrounded by French. Then you'd just fall into it, automatically."

"Automatically," Jimmy mimicked. His beautiful sister thrust out her nonexistent hips and gave him a sultry glance.

"If Mack and Phyllis had a place in France, we would have to row across the Atlantic in a bathtub. That's about all we could afford," his father said, slapping his mother on the rear end. She told him to leave her alone and go do something useful. To Jimmy, she said, "Go play the piano, why don't you." Then, with music filling the kitchen, she made Nathan sit down at the table. "We're going to find a way to make it work. Because a summer in the country, and you can bet any amount of money that Mack and Phyllis's place is really exquisite because I know them, they never do anything halfway, is healthier for you children than a summer cooped up in a hot, dirty city. Believe me." Nathan had looked at her silently. "Cooped up" wouldn't have been the words he would have used to describe it. He saw it as release, a summer of being released into the arteries of the city, a summer of independence.

They went. Judy wrote a letter to the principal unenrolling Nathan in French camp. She put an ad in the paper in Danbury, Connecticut, for a French tutor, and the second day after they arrived at the compound that sat at the end of a dirt road, hidden in a lush and tangled forest, Mlle. Tanguy puttered down the long driveway that linked their cottage to the main house, bumping over the stones in a peculiar-looking car that he discovered later was called a Citroën.

"*Bonjour, Nathan, comment vas-tu? Tu vas bien?*" She spoke to him immediately, getting right to business, not even waiting to shut the rusted door on her car. She leaned into the back seat, brought out paper, books, and a pencil case, and straightened up and looked towards the cottage. He followed her inside, and that whole first lesson he stared at her weathered face as her light, cheerful voice subdued whatever resistance he might have had. *"Comment t'appelles-tu? Tu es Nathan?"*

"Oui," he said lamely and followed her around the cottage as she stuck labels on all of their furniture. On the door to his parents room it said, *"le père, la mère."* On the door to Jimmy's room it said, *"la soeur."* On his door it said, *"le frère."*

For the next week, as he swam and ate and walked the road between their cottage and the main house, his mind was occupied with French. Once he managed to get out of bed, he would find himself making the effort. *Le bateau* was the word he thought of as he and Jimmy pushed the rowboat into the shiny black pond that sat at the bottom of the enormous lawn, and when Jimmy was at the oars and it drifted too close to the willows, forcing them to duck under the trailing leaves, he thought, *l'arbre.* When they entered the darkness underneath the trees, where insects hung in clouds, and frogs they couldn't see plopped into the murky water, all that circled around in his mind was *l'eau.* And when Jimmy would hold the boat still, jamming her oar into the soft mud so they would have to stay there and endure the mosquitoes, he glared at her and thought, *la soeur.* Even though the clammy feeling of the place made his hands sweat, he thought, *il est midi.* Because he didn't know how to add qualities, his mind lost its adjectives and started to focus on the thing in its neutral state, in its perfect beingness. Of course there was the time he got so angry at her, he kicked the oar out of her hand. It flew up and splattered them both with mud. That gave them the idea. The next time, they rowed under the willows purposely and used the oar like a shovel to scoop up the soft mud which *la soeur* patted on her face and legs and arms until she was covered. Nathan didn't like touching the mud so he painted his face, and that was all. Then they rowed back to the dock and lay down in the sun to let it dry. But it didn't dry brown. It dried blue and smelly.

"Haven't you been smelling something?" Jimmy asked, suddenly sitting upright.

"You," he answered. *"La sewer."* He started to laugh. *"La sewer!"*

She dove into the water, staying under until the far side of the pond, where she popped up, her face clean and white, her long, brown hair shiny with wetness. He dove in after her because the smell was pretty terrible and he had been thinking about all of the frog poop that must have settled into the very mud he'd patted on his cheeks.

"La sewer!" he shouted. *"La sewer! La sewer!"* He tried to make her angry, but she only said in her superior tone, "Oh, shut up. You're just a baby."

"I'm a *garçon*," he shouted, kicking water into her face.

But she was a better swimmer than he was, and no amount of splashing would make her falter. She was also a better diver. And she could play the piano and improvise with the dancers in the troupe who were also in residence and, like his parents, planted trees in the morning and lived like guests on the estate the rest of the day. They loved Jimmy and predicted a career for her in modern dance.

Somehow, even though she was two years younger, she had traveled far ahead of him. She had figured out all the connections so that she could move from one accomplishment to another, never even looking like she was working very hard at anything. She had whole strings of connections while he went from one simple noun to another, doomed to the dullness of single words.

Dinners at the main house were formal. First there were cocktails in the living room. The evening sun (*le soleil*) hit the bottles of booze like a dagger, making them glisten at the center of the room. Nathan and Jimmy were each served a small glass of sweet sherry.

Jimmy took hers into the living room and drank it in little sips as she played the piano. All she played, all that summer, was Beethoven's "Für Elise." She'd been able to get it to sound pretty good on their out-of-tune upright at home, but on the grand piano in the dining room of the big house on Mack and Phyllis's estate, it sounded rich and mysterious, and Nathan was amazed every time he heard it. How could it be that simply following a bunch of notes she could make him have such feelings? It was as though Beethoven were talking to him, telling him something he alone needed to hear. So he listened. He listened without appearing to listen. The exasperating thing was that Jimmy liked to play when there was an audience. Her eyes would get a glazed-over look, and she'd sway in and out, her delicate white hands flying over the keys like moths. You almost didn't see them.

Nathan stayed in the living room, studying the design in the Oriental carpet, trying to match it to the design on the sofa. Or he smelled the odor of old fires which wafted out of the enormous fireplace, and tried to balance it with the bits of conversation, or the fan moving above their heads, its black blades whipping the air into a steamy froth. *La conversation.* He couldn't figure out why any of it mattered. Or if it did. And if it didn't, he wanted to know why they bothered. For instance, what was the point of playing music and making someone feel out of control? Nathan walked from the bowl of black olives to the bowl of green olives, to the tray of cheese and crackers, to the bowls of baby corn and tiny gherkins, thinking his thoughts and taking a sample at each stop.

"And how are your French lessons going?" Mack slapped him so soundly between the shoulders, he almost spit out the olive pits he had been storing in his mouth and absently exploring with the tip of his tongue.

"Fine," he said.

"Can you say that in French?"

"*Bien.*"

"Good boy! Well, keep it up! You never know when a foreign language will come in handy. Did I ever tell you I was stationed near Paris at the end of the war?"

"Did you kill anyone?"

"Never had to, but I came damned close a couple of times. You enjoying those olives? Now, if it were up to you, which ones do you think are best, the black or the green? Tell me your honest opinion."

Mack leaned in close to him as though he really wanted to know, and gazing up into his light blue eyes, Nathan saw a flicker of something, a shadow passing where a shadow shouldn't have passed because the man's eyes were so blue and filled with light. Yet something dark had opened up inside them and then closed just as suddenly. There on the rosy, liver-spotted face, something in the eyes, something he shouldn't have seen. And Mack knew that he'd seen it. *Le secret*. Nathan didn't even try to guess what it was.

Estella rang the dinner bell, and they filed into the dining room. Jimmy got up from the piano and joined him at the table. They were placed together between Erik, the drummer, and Molly, a dancer who always wore long flouncy skirts with petticoats underneath them. She also wore mostly unbuttoned blouses and was haphazard about the way she leaned over. For Nathan, meals were a series of hurried glances down the ravine between her breasts.

"Lovely, lovely, lovely," Phyllis sang out, clapping her hands. "The table looks lovely, Estella!"

"Thank you, ma'am," Estella said as she came in with a platter of roasted chicken.

"And it smells heavenly. And Jimmy, your playing sounds more wonderful every day. Aren't we lucky mortals? I'm so glad we're all here together, working and making art, and I feel so lucky to have Mack, and Mack is so lucky to have money." She pouted a little and asked, "You don't mind my saying that, do you, sweetheart?"

Mack answered in a voice made gravely by years of smoking. "I feel that it is my special role as a businessman to be sensitive to the plight of artists. The sacrifices you artists make create a life worth living for the rest of us. You show us beauty, you show us true feeling. And I'm happy to support the arts in whatever small way I can."

"Isn't he a wonderful man?" Phyllis asked the table. "I'm so glad I married you."

"She only married me for my money," Mack said.

"I did, sweetheart, I did. And then I fell head-over-heels."

"Let's have a toast to Mack and Phyllis, who made it possible for all of us to be together." *Le père* said that. He took it upon himself to be master of ceremonies, the liaison between the nobility and peasants.

"As long as you plant those trees!" Mack cried out.

"And make art and make dances," Phyllis added. Then she said, "We are so lucky, all of us, to be here at this wonderful place. And to have your delicious food, Estella."

"Thank you, ma'am."

She was stopping between each of them, holding the heavy

platter of chicken with one hand and serving with the other. Her skin against her crisply starched uniform looked very brown, and her stooped posture, as she bent down between each person, seemed to carry in it the hardships of other times and places. By the time she came between Nathan and Molly, her hand was so unsteady the platter was shaking. Nathan stated his choices quickly so she could move on. That was how he, the one who existed in a world of simple nouns, tried to help her out. But then he noticed that the shaking stopped when she was between Jimmy and Erik, and he saw that Jimmy had put her own hand under the platter to give Estella's hand a rest. She didn't say anything, and Estella didn't say anything, either, and when she moved on to serve the next person, the platter started to shake again.

Erik, the only male in the dance troupe, had straight black hair and an overly serious expression. He wore black tights and a black T-shirt whether they were rehearsing or not, and he seemed particularly solicitous of Jimmy, which made Nathan jealous because Molly ignored him except to lean over and let him gaze down her cleavage.

"How are the trees coming along, Mack?" Erik asked across the table. "Are we on schedule?"

"A bit behind," Mack said. "Tomorrow, we're going to have to start at six o'clock." Nathan looked up and saw the butterfly wing close suddenly in Mack's eye. "We could use a strong kid like you, Nathan. Can you pull him out of bed, Paul? He could handle the water truck. Maybe Jimmy could help Estella in the kitchen."

"Can't I plant trees, too? I'm stronger than Nathan."

"Can you make use of her?" Mack asked Estella, who was coming around with a platter of rice.

"Sure thing, boss. You get here at six o'clock when your brother goes out with the other folks, and I'll put you to work." She smiled at Jimmy, her white teeth shining in the darkness of her face.

Mack was planting Russian olives around the borders of his two hundred acres. It was a small ornamental tree with tiny oval leaves. Barbed wire fencing would have been faster and cheaper, but Mack grew up on a huge ranch in the West, and he wanted the illusion of infinite space, but for practical reasons needed to know where his boundaries were. The tree planting was slow work so Phyllis, Mack's third wife, and formerly an unemployed dancer, conceived the plan of inviting her friends from New York City. She thought of Paul and Judy in Philadelphia when she realized that the smallest cottage would make an ideal studio for a painter and that the garage of the larger cottage would be adequate for Paul's ceramics. The dancers stayed in the guest rooms in the main house, and she gave the cottages to the Bogmores.

The next morning, Nathan was up at five o'clock with everyone else. He put on a grumpy act because he assumed it would be expected, but really, he was pleased to be awake when the sky was just getting light and the woods behind the cottage were full of singing birds. He did what he was supposed to do—he got dressed and ate a bowl of cereal—secretly watching himself go through the routine.

Le père was full of energy, *la mère* was quiet, *la soeur* kept bumping into him as they walked down the road to the main house. Nathan didn't bump her back. There wasn't any need to engage with any of them. Everything around him was shouting, the grass, the sky, the black-eyed Susans growing at the side of the road, and he looked at each thing and, in his mind, told it to shut up. Even the birds. He was happy because it was early in the day, he was awake, and it was clear that the world could be molded and controlled. The birds chirped in a sedate manner now, the wildflowers weren't so brazen. *Les oiseaux, la fleur, le ciel.*

Jimmy went into the big house, the screen door snapping shut behind her. Nathan followed his parents into the barn, where the dancers were already loading the truck with trees. The Russian olives were small and easy to lift, and they'd swing them up to the bed of the truck, standing them on their burlap-wrapped dirt balls. They loaded twenty-five trees, and then they hooked up the wagon for the water drum.

The screen door snapped again, and Mack came out of the house in work clothes and a cowboy hat. He slapped Nathan on the shoulder blades and then showed him how to fill the empty drum from the large tank on the truck. Water was going to be Nathan's responsibility. When the drum was empty, he was the one who'd have to fill it.

Paul rode up front with Mack, and everyone else walked. The

truck went the same pace that they did, smashing down weeds and saplings as it crossed the field and climbed the hill to the spot where they had finished the day before.

La mère was lagging behind, talking to Molly, but then she caught up with Nathan. "Isn't it glorious?"

Phyllis always said glorious. The sky was glorious, the food was glorious, the conversation was glorious. "It's okay," Nathan replied, wanting to lock his feelings away from her prying eyes.

"It hasn't rained yet," she added. "Mack wants it to because the trees really need it. I do, too. I need the day off."

"You only have to work till ten-thirty."

"It's hard, though. You wait and see." She took off her work gloves and held out her hands. "See these?" She pointed to fleshy bumps on her palm. "Calluses. You try shoveling for a couple of hours."

"I'm not going to shovel. I'm going to pull the water wagon."

His mother didn't even acknowledge the challenging tone of his voice. She took off her canvas hat and wiped her forehead. "Even now it's getting hot. Nathan, you didn't wear a hat."

"I'll be okay."

"With the sun beating down on you, you'll get really tired."

"I thought we were going to be in the woods."

"Right, but there'll be flies."

"I'll be okay," he mumbled.

Part of the excitement he felt came from understanding the power of his body. He didn't get cold, and he didn't get hot. Flies didn't bother him. Shoveling, if he had to do it, wouldn't bother him, either, because he could stand almost anything. Hadn't he gone through the entire winter wearing nothing heavier than a sweatshirt? Even during their one snowstorm.

Molly caught up to *la mère* and, sending Nathan a glance, put her hand on his mother's arm. "I'd love to come to your studio sometime and see what you're doing."

"Oh gosh, really? I'm not ready yet. I'm just getting started."

"What are you working on?"

"Well, I thought I'd do a series of paintings of the pond. In fact, I think I'm just going to paint the pond all summer."

Nathan could tell that Molly thought that was a stupid idea because she said "Really?" in a way that sounded false.

But *la mère* didn't notice. "It changes all the time. In the morning if it's sunny, it looks one way, in the evening, it's all dark and mysterious. I saw a deer drinking at it the other evening."

"Wow!" Molly said. "I'll have to pay better attention."

"I've never lived in the country," *la mère* went on, "and everything just seems like a miracle. A raccoon, a deer, even the way the squirrels chatter at you from the trees."

"Tell me something, are you enjoying it?"

"Oh heavens, yes. Anything to get out of the city."

"Do you think it's fair that we should be doing this backbreaking work? An hour or two, I'd be happy to put in. But four and a half hours is exhausting, and frankly, our rehearsals aren't going well because everyone's so tired. You have to be really focused for modern dance. Intention has to inform every movement, and what we've been doing lately has just felt blurred."

"I know it's hard, but Mack's depending on us."

"I'd be happy to do it for a short while."

"And they treat us so well. That wonderful food and a whole cottage to use as a studio."

"Our studio is the lawn, and it slopes," Molly said discontentedly. "You have a cottage to live in and we all have these rather small rooms and mine is right above Mack and Phyllis's and he's got the TV on late every night…I don't know if the man has insomnia or what."

"Excuse me," *la mère* said, "I want to catch Nathan for a minute. Can we talk again later?"

"Sure, but remember, I really would love to see your pond paintings when you're ready to show them."

"Thanks." *La mère* steered Nathan off to the side, right behind the tailpipe. Nathan got a lungful of smoke and coughed it out noisily.

"Are you all right, sweetheart? Listen, I've been wanting to ask you, how's French?"

"Fine."

"Well, say something to me."

"*Le frère.*"

"Let's see, that's 'brother.' Gosh, it's been so long. Well, good, can you say something else?"

"*La soeur.*"

"Oh, I know what that is. 'The sister.'"

"*Très belle.*"

"Sure, I'm starting to remember. 'Very beautiful.' Your sister *is* very beautiful, isn't she? But you're very handsome. Let's see. *Le garçon est...* I don't know the word for handsome."

He didn't, either. It wasn't a word, even in English, he thought about much. Probably because he didn't care if he was handsome or not. Power was what he thought about. But it wasn't power like strong muscles. Another kind of power. A power that lifted him above all of the petty problems of his existence, like flies and hot sun and the necessity to learn another language, to a place somewhere in the atmosphere where all surfaces were smooth, and logic was the supreme order, not feelings.

Even though he hadn't done well in math that year, he had appreciated the systems. All you had to do was set down a system, and then you could use it to answer any number of problems, and each time, if you stuck to the system, you'd get the right answer.

Nathan heard Mack shift the truck into a lower gear as the hill got steeper. The back wheels slipped in the soft dirt, and a couple of the trees fell over.

"When's your next lesson?" *la mère* asked.

"She's coming this afternoon."

"Well, you pay really good attention. Just let go of English and try to melt into the French, okay? If you resist it, it will be that much harder."

"*Oui, maman.*"

"That's my sweetheart. Look, we're getting close. That's where we stopped yesterday."

Mack parked the truck on a level spot, and *le père* jumped out and opened the tailgate. Everyone took a shovel. *Le père* went off with a tape measure and marked the place for each tree and then cut away the undergrowth to clear a spot for the hole. Nathan watched him, waiting for Mack to give him instructions. Soon, he heard the dry sounds of shovels scratching against the hard earth. There wasn't even any dew to wet the surface. The dirt they shoveled up was a light brown in color, mixed with rock, and only when they were down a foot or more did the soil turn damp.

"Nathan, my boy! First, we're going to fill the water drum." Mack didn't look at him, just stooped down and undid the clamps holding the wagon on the trailer. "You wheel it over to the hose. That's a boy. See, it's easy to push when it's empty. But it'll get a little heavy. But not too heavy for you. You're a strong boy. I've been looking at you, I've seen those muscles. Right?"

Mack took his cowboy hat off, and under his white hair, Nathan saw the shadow in his eyes.

He uncoiled the hose from the bed of the truck. It was hooked to a fifty-gallon tank that he had filled at the house that morning. "See, you position it like this." Mack put the nozzle into the top of the water wagon and turned on the spigot. Water ran noisily into the empty container. "Now, the important thing is that you watch it while it's filling because if you don't turn the spigot off when it's full, the water will just spill out, and we can't let that happen. Because when we're out here, this is the only water we've got, and all these little trees are depending on you. They don't get water, they'll die. And I know you don't want that to happen. Now, they'll be digging holes for a while. The ground's hard. Hasn't rained in three weeks. So come over here, and I'll show you something. All right? Want to see something?"

The kind of power Nathan dreamed of was uninvolved power. He might have admired the way Mack ordered everyone around if he hadn't felt a hint of cruelty somewhere. Nathan's power came out of a disinterested involvement, and since logic was its operative, he didn't ever have to manipulate. He followed Mack into a grove of trees. Mack said they were ash.

"Now, look at this, son." Mack pointed to scratches on the bark of one of the trees, places where something had rubbed the bark down to the yellow wood underneath it. "That's made by a buck sharpening his antlers."

"How'd you find it?"

"Oh, I just happened to see it. Yup, a young buck, horny as hell, rubbing his antlers. Go ahead, touch it."

Nathan reached out and touched the damp scar.

"Isn't that something? You stick with Mack, and you'll see some things. A horny young buck, well." The cowboy hat was back on his head. "Us boys are going to stick together." In the leaf-dappled sunlight, caught with the older man between the trees, Nathan felt his hands get moist. The butterfly wings were completely open in Mack's eyes, and Nathan knew he shouldn't look at them closely, even though he could tell, in a side glance, that the designs were beautiful.

That afternoon, he sat at the kitchen table with Mlle. Tanguy. *"Le bateau, le fleuve."* He repeated after her, hearing the easy glide of the words in his mind and knowing they came out halted and sloppy. *"La maison, l'homme, l'arbre."* Those last two he thought he said nicely.

"Très bien!" Mademoiselle said, clapping her hands, her bracelets jingling. *"Nathan, s'il te plaît, un verre d'eau."*

He sat a moment, trying to figure it out.

"Une verre d'eau, s'il te plaît."

Suddenly, he understood, but he stood up so quickly the chair fell backwards. His face went red because Mademoiselle was laughing. *"Maladroit,"* she said.

He wasn't sure what that meant, but he had a pretty good idea. He placed the glass on the table, and she lifted it eagerly to take a sip. "Delicious water. Everyone should drink eight glasses of water a day. Do you know why?"

"No, Mademoiselle."

"Water lubricates all the systems. It does the same thing in your body as oil does in an engine. Do you know what oil does in an engine?"

"It lets all the different parts move."

"That's right. You're a very smart boy. I bet you can't wait till you can drive, can you?"

"I can wait."

"Mon dieu! A boy who isn't anxious to drive! How very unusual!"

The truth was that he hadn't even thought about driving.

"All right, back to *français.* Now, in our first week you've learned many nouns. It's time for review. When I say each word I want you to repeat it after me, write it down, spelling it correctly, and then tell me what it means."

They spent the whole lesson making a list, and when they were done, there were sixty-two nouns. He knew about half of them by heart. The rest he would have to study.

"Next week, I will give you a test."

"A test?"

"A test. And I expect it to be one hundred percent correct. And if it is, we will move on to verbs."

"Mademoiselle, I don't think they give tests in summer school."

"They most certainly do, and therefore we will have a test here." She unzipped her pencil case and took out a freshly sharpened pencil.

"Mademoiselle, what is the word for suspicion?"

"Suspicion? That is an English word I don't know."

"If I am afraid that a person is trying to do something secretly, that's a suspicion."

"Ah, *soupçon*! Should we add that one to the list? You are an unusual boy, Nathan. My nephew, who is one year younger than you, can't wait till he can start to drive, and 'rocket' or 'airplane' or 'battleship,' those are the words he wants me to teach him." She wrote the time and day of their next meeting, then put her pencil back in the case and stood up, her bracelets jingling. "Good boy, study your words, drink eight glasses of water a day, and obey your parents." He walked her to her car, noticing the way the gravel driveway made her teeter in her high heels.

When Jimmy came back from the main house, they fixed themselves big glasses of chocolate milk for lunch and were drinking it on the front steps when *le père* walked up from the garage.

"Hi, kids," he said nonchalantly. "Having fun?"

Jimmy said yup; Nathan said yes.

"Is your mother home yet?"

"She's still at her studio."

"So, what are you two doing this afternoon?"

"Hey, Dad," Nathan said, suddenly realizing that they hadn't done anything together, just the three of them, in a long time, "do you want to come fishing?"

"Fishing?"

Nathan could tell *le père* was trying to think of an excuse to get out of it.

"Are there fishing rods?"

"There's a whole bunch of them in the barn."

"I've got to fire a kiln this afternoon. Let's go another day, all right? I'm going to be too hot to do anything today except jump in for a quick dip. Why don't you and Jimmy go fishing?"

Their father disappeared into the house to make himself some lunch. They stayed on the steps, listening to the sounds coming from the kitchen. They knew he was making his customary peanut butter and banana sandwich and washing a piece of fruit. They also knew it was hopeless to try and get him to come fishing. They didn't say that, they didn't have to. It was enough just to be on the step together, caught in the sound of their father's lunch-making activities. The resentment they both felt slowly disappeared into the heavy trill of the insects.

"Know what I think?" Jimmy was digging her toes into the warm gravel. "I bet they didn't want kids. I bet we were accidents."

"I might have been an accident. But then they realized it wasn't so bad so they decided to have you."

"Yeah, they wanted me, and they only kept you because they couldn't send you back."

"Whatever. Do you want to go fishing?"

"I ain't never done it before."

Their father, who was coming out the front door with a sandwich in his hand, said, "Jimmy, only uneducated people use 'ain't.' Your parents have college degrees, and I don't want to hear it, okay?"

"Okay," she said. She pushed her hair out of her eyes and looked up at Nathan. "You're going to have to teach me how to fish."

"Sure," he said. But he'd only done it once or twice himself, and that was a long time ago.

The two of them walked down the road to the main house. Jimmy had put her sneakers back on, but Nathan had taken his off and was walking barefoot to toughen up the soles of his feet. In the gloomy coolness of the barn, he saw a bunch of fishing rods propped against the back wall. He took down two and handed Jimmy a tackle box he saw in the corner. Then he rummaged around in the gardening shed till he found a trowel.

"What's that for?"

"Bait."

"What're we going to use for bait?"

"I'm going to use worms. You can use whatever you want to use."

By the house, they could hear the music from the lawn where the dancers were rehearsing. When they walked around to the other side, they could see the three women twirling around in brightly colored skirts and then, one by one, dive down onto the grass, their skirts opened around them.

"Don't they look like flowers?" Jimmy asked.

Nathan thought they just looked like girls doing something stupid. Erik came prancing between them, the drum hanging from a shoulder strap so he could drum and dance at the same time.

"So what're you going to do?" Nathan didn't want to look at the dancers anymore.

"Do the worms have to get killed?"

"How else are you going to get them onto the hook?"

"I don't want to kill a worm."

"Fine. Fish with raisins."

"Fish don't eat raisins."

"Right, they don't." Nathan walked around the pond to the darker side where the willows grew, and squatting in the shade under the trees, he dug away at the dirt. Even there it was dry. The worms had to tunnel deep to find any moisture. He dug down to where the earth was black and pungent and picked out five big fat ones. He closed his fist around them and walked over to the dock, where he put them on the wood, and before they could wiggle away, cut each one into thirds. He left the pieces in a clump under the strong sun. Then he took a fishing rod and poked the hook through one of the worm pieces. Stuff came oozing out around the hook, but Nathan didn't notice. Jimmy had walked over to watch. "You want me to put one on your hook, too?"

"I don't want to go fishing."

"Okay. Then all of these worms are going to waste because I can't use them all."

"Well, you were stupid for cutting them all up."

"You were stupid for saying you were going to come fishing if you weren't going to let me put a worm on your hook."

"I'm going to get some raisins."

"But you said yourself, fish don't eat raisins."

"Maybe they do." She ran off towards the main house, and he watched her make a wide arc around the dancers and get swallowed into the shadows of the patio. When she came back, she put a raisin on her hook and cast the way he had done, her line plunking easily into the center of the pond.

"How'd you learn how to cast like that?"

"Estella told me."

"Estella knows how to fish?"

"Yup, but she's never caught anything."

"Then she's a great one to be giving you advice."

"She doesn't fish for fish. She fishes for spirits. The pond goes to the underworld, and if you want to fish, you have to ask the spirits if you can join them."

"Is that what you did?"

She nodded, and when he looked at her skeptically, she said, "You don't have to ask them out loud. You just ask them in your head."

"Whatever." He felt himself floating up to the top of the sky, where nothing Jimmy said had any meaning and where the fact that they sat there, on the end of the dock, the two of them, all afternoon, and fished, he with pieces of worm and she with raisins, and caught nothing at all, and didn't even feel a tug, didn't matter. It was summer, there was nothing to do, and all he knew about was how to go from one thing to another thing, and there was no way that he could see to make any of it string together.

At dinner that night, Jimmy didn't sit next to him. She helped Estella serve. When their mother noticed her absence, she said, "Nathan, where's Jimmy?"

Though he knew she had gone to the kitchen, it didn't seem necessary to tell that to his mother, so he pretended he didn't know. Just then, Jimmy came out with bowls of soup.

"You're serving?"

Jimmy nodded yes happily. Estella had told her how to do it, and she moved around from person to person, leaning over their right shoulder and placing a bowl of soup on their plate.

"When are you going to eat?"

"I'm going to eat in the kitchen," Jimmy said.

"But I don't see you all day long. I really want you to eat with us." She looked at *le père*. "Honey, don't you agree?"

"She should do what she wants."

When Jimmy came out next with a bowl of freshly grated

cheese, which she offered to each guest for their soup, *la mère* said, "Jimmy, don't you want to eat with us?"

"Estella's teaching me how to cook," she said proudly.

When she went back to the kitchen, *la mère* turned to Mack and Phyllis and said, "I hardly see her. I really want to have her with us at dinner."

"This is part of her job," Mack said. "You'll have her all night, Judy."

"And look at her," Phyllis added. "She's so happy to have the responsibility."

That night Mack invited them all into the living room for after-dinner drinks. Nathan and Jimmy each got sherry. Jimmy was heading into the dining room to practice the piano when Phyllis said, "Jimmy, dear, you know we love to hear you play, but tonight I wanted to put on some records. Just for a change."

"Come here, sweetheart," their mother called. "I want to talk to you." She held out her arms, and when Jimmy came over, *la mère* gave her a long hug. "So what did you do this morning with Estella?"

"I helped her chop up vegetables."

"That was all?"

"She showed me how to make a pie crust."

"You mean that delicious pie crust was yours?"

"With Estella's help."

"Oh, honey, I'm so proud of you. It was so light and flaky. Really terrific. Gosh, when we get back home, maybe you can teach me. I'm such an old poop at baking."

Suddenly, dance music filled the living room. Phyllis grabbed Mack, and the two of them swung around, arm in arm, like people in a movie. Erik chose Natalie, and they moved around the room in dramatic movements that included a lot of swooping and twirling. *Le père* and *la mère* shuffled around in each other's arms with smiles plastered on their faces, and Molly came over to Nathan. "Put down your glass, and I'll teach you how to do it."

He froze up right away because he couldn't imagine how he could ever fit against her without crushing into her boobs. But Molly seemed very comfortable with the idea and put his left arm around her waist and his right arm around her neck. He stood a foot out from her body as she steered him into the center of the room. "Just do what I do. And relax. You feel as stiff as a piece of cardboard."

But all Nathan wanted was to get back to his glass of wine. Her perfume was suffocating him, and her bosom, which she pushed against him, closing up the distance, felt dangerous. Also, he was certain he was going to step on her toes.

"Loosen up," Molly whispered. "I'm not going to bite you. Now, lift your arm up. I'm going to twirl around. There. That wasn't so hard, was it? Now, you twirl."

He wobbled around and managed to find her on the return.

"Well, okay. A little stiff, because you're moving like a robot, but not bad. You know what you should do? You should come out on the lawn with us. Try some improvising. You're not trusting your body. And you need to learn to trust it. Tomorrow afternoon, why don't you come out?"

The song ended, and Molly released him. Nathan went back to his glass, but afraid that someone else would make him dance, he didn't stay in the living room. He went into the kitchen looking for Jimmy. But the kitchen was dark. Still holding his glass, he went outside. There was a soft breeze, a scent of freshly cut grass, and animals singing in the distance, insects, frogs, he didn't know exactly. Above the barn he saw a light on in the small apartment Estella had. There were steps cut into the hillside, and at the top, the door was partly open. But he couldn't tell if Jimmy was in there or not.

"I found two of my best fishing rods down at the dock this morning," Mack said at dinnertime the next day. "Now…" He paused, looked around the room at each of them. "I consider all of you my guests. And as guests, you are entitled to make use of all the equipment, which includes a rowboat, a canoe, fishing rods, lifejackets, wading boots, the golf cart, the jeep. But anything you use I expect you to return in good condition to the spot you found it in. That's just my little rule. Maybe it doesn't make sense. There wasn't much dew this morning, and the fishing rods probably weren't hurt by being outside, but when I saw them I had to ask myself who would be so careless with equipment that didn't belong to them."

Estella came in with a platter of roast lamb. Jimmy followed her with two bowls, one of mint jelly, one of gravy. They served Mack first, and when his plate was full, he put his napkin on his lap and looked up at them and said, "Well, I'm sure you'll all respect my wishes. Even Nathan and Jimmy, right?"

"I'm sorry, sir," Nathan said. "I left them out. I just forgot."

"I left mine out, too," Jimmy said. "We won't do it again."

"Now that's impressive," Phyllis said to Mack.

"They're good kids," Mack said offhandedly. "Good kids."

Their mother and father were smiling. Everyone was smiling.

Molly, as though she were oblivious to what was going on, broke in with, "This is such tasty lamb, so tender."

Phyllis called, "Estella, you're getting compliments! Everyone loves your lamb!"

"Thank you," Estella called back. Jimmy appeared with a tureen of peas. She went to Mack first, but he waved her away, saying, "I'm a healthy man, Jimmy, and peas are the one vitamin pill I don't take."

On Friday Nathan scored one hundred on Mademoiselle's test on nouns. That afternoon she started him on verbs by asking him which ones he wanted to learn. She handed him a fresh pencil from her pencil case, and he wrote down the first five that came to mind: to swim, to row, to walk, to dance, to worry.

"Does a boy who is your age like to dance?" Mademoiselle asked. He said that he hated to dance.

"That is another one, to hate. Do you like to walk?"

"No," he told her, he hated it more than dancing.

"Then what do you like to do?" she asked.

He looked at her hard, angular chest, trussed up behind the shiny fabric of her blouse, and said that he liked to fish.

"Ah, fish, all boys like to fish. Every time you fish, you think, *pêcher*. Tell me about the biggest fish you ever caught."

"I don't catch any."

"Ah, be patient. That is the answer to everything."

It was true. And patience was something that Nathan knew how to practice. At that moment, for instance, he was waiting for answers to several questions that had developed over the two weeks they'd been at Mack's place. The first was about Mack himself. What did he want with Nathan? The second had to do with Estella. What was she teaching Jimmy? The third was, when would disaster strike?

Nathan was fond of catastrophes: train wrecks, airplane crashes, hurricanes, tornadoes. One moment everything was its normal boring self, and the next moment the world was skewed to a weird angle, and there was nothing familiar anywhere. Such amazing changes woke everybody up and gave them new energy. Because as he saw it, everyone was drifting off to sleep, forgetting to pay attention. His mother was painting ponds in her studio all day long. His father was making vases. The dancers were improvising on the lawn. According to Erik, they were stretching the limits of their bodies and experimenting with organic form. But when Nathan looked at them, he thought they were just out there trying to be children again and looking stupid in the process.

Meanwhile, the world was drying up around them. The pond was evaporating, the dirt was crusting over, the leaves on everything were going brown. Grasshoppers were everywhere, clicking in and out of the dry grasses, and any fish that knew their business were hanging out down at the bottom of the pond, away from heat and fishermen and sunlight.

And Mack. Mack was taking him off to the forest every morning. Jimmy was spending more and more time up in the apartment over the barn with Estella. And sometimes she stayed with her in the kitchen after dinner, helping her to clean up. Nathan was on a campaign to be nice to *la soeur* because if she disappeared completely, there would be no one out there at all.

That morning after he'd dragged the water wagon to every tree they'd put in over the last three days and given them such a long drink the big tank on the truck was halfway down, he'd gone back to wait until they were finished planting the new ones. He was also waiting for Mack, who had gone down to inspect the trees they'd put in last week.

When he came up to Nathan, he was breathing heavily, and his face under the wide brim of the cowboy hat was as red as a piece of raw meat. "Come here, son, there's something back in here I want to show you."

Nathan followed him into an area of the forest where there were trees with thin, shaggy trunks standing against the sky like prison bars. Mack squatted down and pushed some leaves away from a low green plant with small pink blossoms. "See this here. This is herb Robert. It grows in the shade, and it looks delicate, but herb Robert can withstand a lot of tough weather conditions before it gives up. A pretty little plant. Makes good medicine. Helps with anything that ails you. Anything. Well, let's sit down here next to herb Robert." He plopped down to the ground heavily, took off his cowboy hat. "Tell me, Nathan, is there anything you want that maybe your parents won't buy for you?"

Nathan looked up in surprise.

"Hell, that's not such an unusual question. Money's tight, I know that. Your dad doesn't make a lot. I'm a businessman, he's an artist. It's how the world works. And it's not fair, but the truth is that I've got more than I can use, and maybe there's something expensive, or maybe that your parents don't approve of, that you would like to have."

"That's very nice of you," Nathan said.

"Do you have a good bike? I never see you riding a bike."

"I don't particularly like bike riding," Nathan said.

"How 'bout I get you your own professional fishing rod? You'd like that."

"Well, you have so many here already, and I don't have a place to fish at home."

"Yeah, that's right. Well, then, what about...let's see. Maybe I can buy you your first suit. Custom-fit by my tailor. Now that's something."

"Well..." Nathan looked at the ground. "I guess I would feel bad that I was getting something and Jimmy wasn't."

Mack moved in closer. Now he was sitting right on top of herb Robert.

"You're crushing the flower," Nathan said.

"What? Oh, doesn't matter, it's just a plant, there's millions of them, right? Now..."

"It will heal what's ailing you," Nathan said quietly.

"Maybe so, but listen to me, son, I'm going to tell you a little secret. When I was your age, I thought about girls a lot. Know what I mean? Every kid your age is curious. Maybe you'd like some pictures to look at. Would you like that?"

Nathan didn't say anything, so Mack went on. "Naked girls.

Haven't you ever seen them? Now, I'm not talking about your mother or your sister. I'm talking about women showing you everything a boy wants to see, and naked guys, too. When I was your age, I had this uncle, and he did things like that for me, things like I would like to do for you. I could special-order these pictures, see, and they'd be here in two days, and we'd find a hiding place where you could keep them. Would you like that? And how about a bunch of candy bars and some bottles of soda, because I know your mother doesn't let you have that stuff. Your old uncle takes care of you, right? So is that a deal, girlie pictures and guy pictures? Doesn't matter to me, you can have both. And soda. Our little secret. Want to shake on it?"

Nathan put his hands in his pockets and said, "That's okay."

Mack looked at him straight on, his eyes opened wide in the shade, everything that had been hidden before right there in plain sight. He touched Nathan on his knee, and Nathan drew back. "Well, give me a hand up," Mack said.

As they walked out of the forest, Mack put his arm around Nathan's shoulder. It sat up there like a piece of concrete, making him go stiff. When they reached the field, Nathan ducked out from underneath it and ran off into the trees.

That afternoon he asked Jimmy if she wanted to go in the boat with him. She said okay, as long as he didn't fish because she couldn't bear it if he cut up any more worms. There was still a pile of worm crud on the dock from the ones he'd left there after the last time. Nathan squatted down to see how they had decomposed. They didn't look like worms at all anymore, more like smush. So that's what happened when everything in you dried out; you were just a hollow piece of dried-up nothing.

Jimmy pushed the boat into the water, and Nathan stepped down into it from the dock, trying to do it in such a way that wouldn't make it tip. But it did, and Jimmy had to grab onto the sides to keep from sliding out. "Don't ever do that again," she said. "You could have made me spill right over."

He apologized because he wanted her to like being with him. "Let's go over to the willows," he suggested, because he knew she liked floating in the darkness under the leaves.

"No, let's stay out in the open for a while."

He let her row, and she steered them out to the middle of the pond.

"Where's the underworld?" he asked.

She was hanging off the side of the boat, her fingers trailing in the water. "It's underneath us."

"What's in it?"

"All the spirits."

"What spirits?"

"All the spirits of the trees and the animals and the plants."

"So what are they down there for? I mean, what does it matter to us?"

"Lots," she said secretly.

"Come on, Jimmy, tell me."

"I don't know if Estella wants me to tell anybody else. It's sort of special. You can't just tell anybody."

"You can tell me. I'm your brother. And I know something about it, too."

"What do you know?"

"I know about this weed called herb Robert that can cure anything that's the matter with you and it grows in the shade and it has a little pink blossom."

"Where does it grow?"

"Near where they've been planting the trees."

"Show me, okay?"

"I will if you tell me."

Jimmy sat up on the bench and hooked her hair behind her ears. In a different tone of voice she said, "See, how it works is they're down there to help us. What you have to do is dive down into the pond, all the way down, and then you have to find an animal to take you into the underworld."

"Yeah, and you drown in the process."

"I don't have to tell you any of this."

"I'm sorry. I really want to know, okay? I'm sorry."

"You don't dive down for real. You do it in your imagination. It's like playing a made-up game. And when you get to the underworld, you can ask a plant or a tree, whoever comes up to you, for help with your problem. We've been doing it a lot, Estella and me, up in her bedroom. Erik's drumming outside, and the drumming helps us to stay focused."

"I have a problem."

"Okay, tell me, I'll go to the underworld tomorrow with Estella."

"I can't tell you."

"What's it about, then?"

"It's about Mack."

"What happened?" Jimmy asked, suddenly worried.

"Nothing happened, and nothing's going to happen." Suddenly, he didn't trust anything Jimmy was saying. "How do you know Estella's not playing a big joke on you? She's just a cook, she probably never even finished high school."

"You don't have to be educated to know things. And she knows things because she grew up in Jamaica."

"She's from New York. I heard Mack talking about her. She lives in Brooklyn."

"Yeah, but she lived in Jamaica when she was a little girl."

"So, that doesn't mean anything."

"Well, you don't have to believe in it, Nathan. And if I do, that's my business." She picked the oars up and rowed them towards the swampy side of the pond. She didn't go far into it, though; she stopped before the water got too shallow. Nathan could touch the cattails. He saw a bird's nest among them and craned his head to see if there were any eggs. He caught a spot of blue, startling against the dull colors of the rushes. It was a blue as intense as Mack's bloodshot eyes.

"It hasn't rained in four weeks," Jimmy said.

"I know. I'm the one who has to water all those trees."

"Mack's worried."

"Who cares?"

"You might not like Mack, but you can care about the trees, at least."

"They're his trees, why should I?"

"Estella's going to ask the spirits to help the trees."

"I'm sure she is."

"Don't be sarcastic. She's going to ask them to bring rain."

"Rain happens when the right atmospheric conditions are present. And when they are present, it will rain. And it won't if they're not there."

"Do you know something? You're ignoring something very obvious. What people think affects the world. What they want affects the world. What they ask for . . . if they ask for it hard enough, it will happen."

"Sure. I want a car, and a car's going to appear."

"You have to really want it, and it has to be a natural thing, like rain."

"So what if there isn't a natural thing that I want? I'm not ever going to get anything?"

Jimmy ignored his question. "I want rain. Estella wants rain. The trees want rain. It's going to rain."

He looked at her with hatred.

"Not for Mack," she added. "I want rain for the trees."

That afternoon when Mademoiselle came, she asked him to write down fifteen verbs as quickly as possible. As he did it, she went to the sink and filled two glasses with water. She put one in front of him and sat down across from him and drank hers.

"Quickly, quickly, we have much to do." He pushed the paper across to her. She looked at his words and then wrote the French beside the English. When she was done, the list looked like this:

> to swim—nager
> to follow—suivre
> to suspect—soupçonner
> to laugh—rire
> to cry—pleurer
> to dive—plonger
> to find—trouver
> to worry—se tracasser
> to row—ramer
> to watch—regarder
> to fear—craindre
> to fall—tomber
> to give up—abandonner
> to refuse—refuser
> to kick—donner un coup de pied

"This is just a little test I do with all my students. *Une évaluation psychologique.* Okay?" She put a check besides "suspect," "cry," "worry," "be afraid," "fall," "give up," "refuse," "kick." "Eight negatives. Seven positives. You are borderline, Nathan. That is, there is much that is on your mind, and it threatens to overtake your happiness, but it hasn't yet. I suggest to you to have more fun. It will help with the worry, the suspicion, the fear. Right? And you mustn't feel bad about it. Everyone worries, everyone suspects, everyone is afraid. It is human nature. Brush those feelings aside and have fun. If it is French you are worried about, you are an excellent student, a brilliant student. Just keep studying your words, and you'll be fine. Next time if you have learned all of the verbs, I will bring you a reward. That is something you can look forward to, yes?"

The screen door opened, and *le père* walked in. His pants were covered with clay and he tracked clay across the floor. "Hi, Nathan! *Bonjour...*"

Nathan could tell that *le père* had intended to say the French teacher's name but then discovered that he no longer remembered what it was.

"If you'll excuse me, I'm just going to make myself a sandwich, and then I'll be out of your way."

Nathan couldn't concentrate as long as *le père* was in the room. He hoped that he wouldn't be too obvious about the kind of sandwich he was making. Peanut butter and banana would strike a French woman as being pretty weird. Add to it, *le père's* ragged clothes and his goofy good humor. Nathan wanted a father who was a vice president of some big company that made things nobody understood the uses for, someone who wore suits, who drove to work in the morning and didn't return till dinnertime, who made a lot of money, who looked responsible. Nathan glanced at the counter and saw the banana skin lying there in plain view next to the jar of peanut butter. Mademoiselle, meanwhile, was pronouncing each word on the list and pausing for him to repeat it after her. *Pleurer. Plonger. Nager. Ramer.* He noticed that what Mademoiselle called his positive verbs had to do with water.

Jimmy played "Für Elise" during cocktails. Each evening when she sat down at the piano, he would think, Not again! But then the song would start, and no matter how aloof he tried to be, the music pulled him in. It was so melodious, so rich and dark, so full of all his hidden feelings, he had to listen. The piece was a perfect balance of logic and emotion. Maybe all music was that way. Well, he knew one thing for sure. Dance was only emotion. Painting was only emotion. That's why they weren't pure art like music.

People had moved onto the patio because it was so hot. Nathan went outside, too. He stood against the cool wall of the house close to the window so he could continue to listen. No one else paid any attention. *La mère,* sitting across from him, was laughing loudly. She wore a pink dress with a ruffled neckline, and her bare arms, freckled from the sun, were pretty. Molly was laughing, too. Her blouse was unbuttoned so far down he could see her bosom looking at him straight on. Natalie was standing in a corner talking in an animated way with Erik. She had very white skin and dark hair, and there was something quick and silvery about her, she flashed in and out. Nathan tried to imagine her having sex with Erik. He pictured a billowing, a glistening, a rising of bodies that happened simultaneously, as though they were both listening to the same melody in their heads. It would get louder, they would rise higher and higher, and then finally it would burst just as it did now on the piano. The piece ended, there was a pause, and then a little bit later, the opening measure sounded again. Molly put down her drink and, saying "Excuse me" to *la mère,* went into the house. Nathan pulled himself away from the wall and followed her. What if she knew he was following her and had ducked into an empty bedroom to wait for him, and when he came after, she closed the door and turned to face him, her blouse open all the way down? Nipples was a subject he hardly dared to think about.

She stopped at the olives, took some, and then went into the dining room. He stayed back in the shadows, but at a spot where he could see her waving her arms to get Jimmy's attention. But Jimmy was in the song. Her eyes were closed, her body was sloshing in and out. "Jimmy!"

Molly broke the trance. Jimmy looked up, and the music stopped. Molly's nipples would be large and pink. He would want to put his tongue on them.

"Excuse me?" Jimmy said in a startled tone.

"Don't you know any other songs? I mean, is this one the only one you can play?"

"No," Jimmy said defensively.

"Well, then, why don't you give us all a break and play something else for a while."

Jimmy looked at her uncomprehendingly. Then she simply started the song where she had stopped, staring at Molly until she turned around and went out.

By that time, Nathan was sitting on the couch. "Hi!" he said in a friendly way.

Molly gave him an annoyed look. Then she took her olive pits out of her mouth and put them in the ashtray.

"I bet you don't know what I am."

"No, I guess not."

Nathan looked at her smugly, daring himself to go on. "I'm a brilliant student, a brilliant student of love. Would you be my teacher?"

Molly went out, the screen door slamming behind her.

Because it was so hot Estella served a light meal. There were salads and thinly sliced bread and cold cuts. Jimmy brought everything out to the sideboard in the dining room, and everyone helped themselves. Phyllis said, "Mack, why should we sit in here? We'll be much cooler if we eat outside."

"There's only two tables, Phyllis. It won't be very comfortable."

"The kids can put their plates on their laps, can't they? Do you want to do that, Nathan?"

"Sure."

"Jimmy?"

"Jimmy's in the kitchen with Estella."

"Oh, right, I forgot."

"I'm ready," Erik said suddenly and stood up with his napkin and plate. Everyone else followed him outside.

The patio looked out over the lawn that tumbled down to the willows and the pond. Nathan pulled his chair to the edge of the patio and looked at the view. Behind him, he heard *la mère* say to Mack and Phyllis, "You need some swans on that pond and some peacocks strutting around with their tails open."

"Then you've got bird droppings," Mack said.

"Sweetie, Judy wasn't being serious. She was just talking about fantasy. No one wants you to actually go out and do it. Everyone's very happy with just the way things are."

"Well, there is one thing," Judy said.

"What is it? Tell me. You know I'm always looking for suggestions." That was Phyllis.

"Next summer, if you do this again, how about inviting a couple of musicians and a writer or two?"

"Terrific idea! A regular artist colony. Right here in West Redding, Connecticut. The only problem is the musicians. We'd have to build them studios in the woods, otherwise they'd disturb the writers."

"And then at the end of the summer," *la mère* went on, "everyone could do a grand collaboration."

"A piece of cacophonous nonsense," *le père* added.

"Nonsense it might be," *la mère* agreed, "but it would be fun."

Nathan remembered Mademoiselle's advice to him to have more fun. The word was meaningless. It was one of those trick words like happy. If you thought about fun or happiness, it meant that you weren't feeling the real thing. The real thing happened only if you were unaware of it. He looked down at the pond and realized there was movement at the end of the dock. Was it Natalie and Erik? He looked back on the patio and saw them sitting at a table with Molly.

He turned back to the pond and saw a large white bird gliding over the water. "Mom!" he called.

But *la mère* was laughing at something Phyllis had said. Her cheeks were as pink as her dress, and by the time she had finished and Nathan looked out at the pond again, the bird was gone. He could see who was down there now. It was Jimmy with someone in a chair next to her, whom he assumed was Estella. He wondered if they'd seen the bird, too. For a moment, he thought about running down there to tell them about it, but then he noticed their heads were almost touching and they seemed to be deeply involved in whatever they were doing, so he decided to stay where he was.

On most nights, it started to cool down by nine o'clock. But that evening, it seemed to get hotter. Phyllis brought out candles on footed candle sticks and set them around the patio. There were two games of cards going. *Le père* pulled a chair up next to Nathan. "Nice place, isn't it?" he said. "I was so embarrassed today. I couldn't remember your French teacher's name. Do you think she noticed? What is it, anyway?"

"Mlle. Tanguy."

"Tanguy. Well, I'll try to get it right next time."

"It's okay, I don't think she noticed."

"So how's it going?"

"Fine."

"Do things seem familiar? Is she covering the same sorts of things you got in school?"

"Oh, much more."

"And are you paying attention and studying?"

"Yes."

"Good, because we're paying her a good salary. I'll tell you something, this French isn't coming to you cheap."

"If I went to summer school back home, it would be free."

"Summer school? Are you still wishing you were going to summer school? Do you know how hot it is in Philadelphia right now? You think this is bad. And you can swim here and fish and boat, and you and your sister are free to do whatever you want all day long. It seems to me you're just about the luckiest kid in the world."

"I know, Dad."

But that didn't satisfy his father because he went on. "When I think back to the summers I spent in Cleveland when I was your age, living in an apartment, no place to swim...You're in a paradise, thanks to Mack and Phyllis. You know that?"

"Yes, Dad."

"So take advantage, kid."

The moon came up over the willows, a yellow lamp hanging in the darkness. The bullfrogs croaked down at the pond, and all around them in the grass, insects sang.

"Last one in's a rotten egg!" Erik called. He ran across the patio, Natalie behind him.

A few moments later there were splashes in the water. "Hey, it's nice!" Natalie called.

"Are they going skinny-dipping?" Molly asked the people on the terrace.

Nathan ran down the lawn in his bare feet. The pond was a bowl of moonlight. The frogs had gone silent, and he could hear Natalie call, "Over here, I'm over here!" Nathan stepped onto the dock and slipped out of his clothes. He was careful to leave them in a pile separate from the others so he'd be able to find them again. "No, silly, over here." The air felt good on the tender parts of his body. Bits of grass had stuck to his bare feet. He rubbed them on the dry wood to get them off. Suddenly there was a lot of splashing in the water and laughter. He wondered if Jimmy was in there, too. "Watch out, everybody," he called, "I'm diving in!"

The brilliant student of love's pubescent body knifed through the moon, scattering it into fragments. "Is that you, Nathan?" Jimmy asked. She swam over to him, her disembodied face floating on the surface of the water.

"Did you see that bird swooping over the pond?" he asked her.

"You saw it, too?"

"Yeah, it was amazing."

"Not so loud," Jimmy whispered. Her eyes looked enormous. He plinked a little water in her direction and in a low voice said, "What was it?"

"Just Estella. See…" Jimmy pointed up at the lawn, and Nathan saw the same great white form crossing it at the top. "It's her uniform, it glows."

"But it looked like it was out in the middle of the water."

"It looked like it was because you were seeing it with your imagination. That's the best way to see everything." Suddenly she flipped back and floated away from him.

"Hey!" he called after her. He had no idea where Natalie or Erik were, and suddenly there were another three splashes into the pond. People were paddling towards him. He swam away quickly because he hated them all and the only one he wanted to be with was Jimmy. "Jimmy!" he whispered.

"Over here," she said from the direction of the willows.

"Wait for me!" he cried.

"I'll wait, but hurry."

He moved across the water without making a sound and got away from the other people. "Jimmy?"

"Come in closer," she whispered, "but you have to be very quiet."

He saw her white arm on top of the water and swam towards it. She reached out and pulled him in. Then he saw her face, her blue lips, her black eyes, strings of hair. "If we stay very still, the frogs'll start singing again. But we have to be very still."

"Those guys out there are making a racket."

She put her finger to her lips. "Shh! They'll go away soon, and the frogs will think we went with them. Just be quiet."

His penis was so shriveled from the cold water it was no bigger than his pinkie. He was a nothing, worse than a nothing. Jimmy looked at him steadily. He realized he trusted her more than he trusted anyone else in the world. So he stayed there next to her. They must have hung there, just outside the branches of the willows, treading water for half the night. The voices at the other end went away eventually. He heard laughter on the lawn. "You're wearing my shirt!" someone cried. After that, the sounds died away. Sometime later, he wondered if *le père* and *la mère* were back at the cottage, and if they had noticed their children were gone. Maybe they'd come searching with flashlights. They'd make so much noise the frogs would never start singing again. He was about to suggest to Jimmy that they give up. But then he heard a croak. And then another one. Soon there was croaking all around them, then there was trilling, then there was peeping. All the frogs were singing into the night, the bullfrogs, the peepers, the toads. The amphibian population was sawing away at the edges of a pond they assumed was empty, and he and Jimmy were suspended together in the middle of it. Her fingers snaked over the water and found his, and they held hands and listened.

Later, much later, when even the moon was covered over by a cloud, they climbed back onto the dock. They put on whatever clothes they could find and didn't even try to look for their shoes, but started up the lawn barefoot. When they reached the big house the candles were still burning on the patio, and there were voices, hardly audible against the sounds of the night. Nathan heard Mack's gravely laugh. He knew that in another step they'd throw out shadows, so he grabbed Jimmy by the wrist and pulled her away. They started to laugh when they got to the barn. Nathan led Jimmy out to the grassy circle inside the curve of the driveway, and they both lay down inside it.

"I hate Mack," Nathan said.

"Why?"

"He wants to buy me magazines." He knew that wouldn't make any sense to Jimmy, so he added, "So I can look at naked girls."

Jimmy laughed. "What's so bad about that?"

"He's creepy."

"He's nice to me."

"That's because he doesn't want to have sex with you."

Jimmy was quiet. He didn't know if she understood how a man could have sex with a boy, but it didn't matter. The thing was said, and he felt better.

"I went to the underworld. I talked to the willow tree, and a frog was my messenger."

"How'd you do that?"

"In my imagination."

"But Jimmy, maybe it's all made up, then."

He could tell he'd disappointed her because she said in a defensive tone, "It is, and it isn't. It just has to do with what you want to believe."

"So do you believe it?" he asked, afraid of what her answer would be.

"I do. I never doubted anything. Not even from the very beginning."

"So what does it mean? I mean, what difference does it make?"

Jimmy said simply, "I think it means that people aren't the only ones in the world who can feel things."

"Oh great," Nathan replied, but as soon as the words were out of his mouth he regretted it.

That night, there was drumming in his sleep. Erik was just outside the window, calling to him with his drum. Nathan wanted to keep sleeping, but the sound was hypnotic, and he was soon climbing out of the window to join him. Natalie, Molly, and Jimmy were dancing in the darkness. They made a circle around him, and then they reached for his hand. With Erik at the lead, they snaked in and out of the trees. Nathan wasn't thinking about anything; he was just moving to the sounds, noticing every so often how loose and relaxed he felt. Then he was with Jimmy, and they were diving off the dock into the pond. He opened his eyes underwater and followed his sister's naked body down into the grass at the bottom. An oak tree grew down there. Jimmy said, "Hello, oak tree. I'd like to come to the underworld. Would you send me an escort?" A red fox ran up, and Jimmy got onto its back and disappeared. Nathan stayed by the tree. After a while it seemed apparent that an escort wasn't going to come for him. Finally the tree broke the silence, and in a voice that matched his father's, it said, "Don't you know, son, nothing comes without the asking."

"I can ask," Nathan said, and he looked into the watery darkness and asked, "Please, can you send me an escort?"

"You can ask," the tree replied, "but asking only works if it's something you truly want."

The next morning the sky was green. At first the sun shone weakly, but then it was covered over by white clouds. The air was very humid. As his parents and the dancers dug holes for the trees, the shovels clanked against the rocks loudly. Nathan was pulling the wagon along the row of already-planted trees, giving each one a good drink. The tiny leaves were the same green as the sky. They were starting to yellow, particularly on the trees that were planted earlier in the summer, so Nathan gave those the most water. He squatted down and nestled the hose right into the roots. "There," he said, "you'll like that. That's just what you want. Isn't that good? Yes, that's just what you've been missing." He hardly realized he was talking to them, it just came out of his mouth each time as he dug a little hole for the hose to go down into. He counted to three hundred and then he planted the hose into a new tree. The water spilled over his sneakers, pooled in crevices of hard dirt. Leaves and blossoms floated on top of it. Then something caught his eye. A flicker of a different color. It was white and out of place. Mack's white shirt appeared and, above it, the raw meat of his jowls.

"Who're you talking to, Nathan?"

"Nobody."

"But I just heard you say something. Who were you talking to, my boy?"

"Myself."

Mack chucked him on the shoulder. "Well, guess what, kid, I've got something for you." Mack reached into a paper bag and pulled out a thin glossy magazine. "This is yours."

"No thank you."

Water was carrying away the peat moss that had been laid around the base of the tree.

"You don't know what you're missing." Mack flung the magazine open, and there on the ground was Molly's bright pink body, completely unbuttoned and bare. He saw the nipples and the mysterious place he had always wondered about, and as he looked at her, he noticed the changes inside of him.

"You can put your hand on her, Nathan." Mack took his fingers and guided them to the very spot he had been looking at. He hardly noticed what Mack was doing or that the hose was running over his leg. He knew he was touching a picture, a stupid picture, so it wasn't a big deal. But still he wanted to. He wanted to feel it with his whole body, he wanted to pull his pants off and roll around on top of it. He wanted to put the picture into his mouth and eat her. He smelled something. Mack's tongue was moving around in his ear, and his hand was on Nathan's thigh, but what he smelled was the pungent scent of the earth as the water moistened it. Mack's hand was in his crotch, making him so hard he was afraid he was going to explode. Then Mack started to unzip his pants, but the zipper didn't move. It must have been jammed. Mack tried again. Nathan looked at the beefy fingers fumbling at his hips, and right then, just as the man finally got the zipper to go down, he felt himself ejaculate. He was so embarrassed he slapped the hands away and jumped up. The hose caught on his foot and flipped up into Mack's lap. Mack cursed as the water gurgled over his clothes, but Nathan didn't hear anything, he was streaking through the woods, running like a scared child. He ran past the planters, past the truck, and then ducked back into the woods and made his way down the hillside. When he reached their cottage, the first thing he did was run into the bathroom. He ripped off his clothes and stood in the shower in his underwear, letting the water run as hot as he could stand. Then he peeled the drawers off his body and, leaving the shower running, stuffed them in the trash can under the kitchen sink. He ran back through his wet footprints, got back into the shower, and soaped and shampooed vigorously. But once he was clean and rinsed off, he stayed there, under the water.

By the time Mademoiselle arrived, he was dressed and the floor was wiped up and the trash can under the sink was empty because he'd dumped the entire contents into the incinerator.

"Did you study your verbs, Nathan?"

He gave her the list and was able to pronounce each one correctly.

"*Très bien!* Now I will give you my reward!"

He had forgotten about the reward, and when she took out a paperback book written in French with a title he didn't understand, he said, *"Merci, Mademoiselle."*

"We will start reading this soon, once you've finished your sentences. What's it called? Can you tell me?"

"Le Chien d'Anton."

"And what does that mean? Eh? Do you know?" When he didn't respond she said, "Well, we haven't done the animals, so I will tell you. The dog of Anton. Anton's dog. It is a story about a lost dog and how a boy who doesn't have a mother finds him. It is a very sweet story. I give it to all of my students. Now, you know nouns, you know verbs, next we will put them together with connecting words and make sentences. Once you see how to make a sentence, we can really talk to one another."

She wrote "I am" and then left a blank. "Very quickly, I want you to write as many words as you can think of to finish this. For instance, 'I am tired' could be one." She pushed the paper over to him. She had written "tired" in the blank.

He just looked at it stupidly.

"This is so easy, so *facile,* Nathan. Quickly do it, five or six more words."

So he wrote:

> I am lost.
> I am hot.
> I am curious.
> I am lumpy.
> I am stretched.

"Okay." She looked at the list of words but didn't say anything, only printed the French above his English. "Now 'I am' is *je suis.* So each of these sentences begins with *je suis.* Some of these don't make too much sense, but if they are the words you want, okay. For instance, what does 'I am lumpy' mean? Eh? 'I am stretched'? It doesn't make sense. So I have given you what I think you may mean. Okay, now let's think of some ordinary sentences that begin with *je suis. Je suis affamé. Je suis beau. Je suis un homme. Je suis un frère.*"

By the time Mademoiselle was ready to leave, the sky had darkened. "It looks like rain," she said when Nathan walked with her to the Citroën. He stood on the driveway, watching her disappear down the road. When he went back into the house, *le père* waved at him from the garage.

The novel sat on the kitchen table. He carried it into his room and hid it under his underwear in the top dresser drawer.

When he stepped back outside, the sky was the color of lead. Wind shook the tops of the birches, blew the leaves to their undersides. He had to push into the wind as he walked down the road. He wanted to find Jimmy. But if she was in the main house he'd have to get her attention through a window. He didn't want to risk running into Mack. The rain started as he ran down to the pond. No Jimmy. He slammed through the bathhouse, but they never went there, and she wasn't there then. Then he ran back up the lawn and swung behind the main house to the barn. It was pouring steadily, water pulsing out of the gutters, flooding the driveway. The tempo increased. A sheet of gray water hung down from the sky, obliterating everything. He ran up the steps at the side of the barn and pounded on Estella's door at the top. Water spilled off the roof onto his head. Lightning cracked in the sky. He tried the knob because he didn't think anyone could hear him in that racket, and the door opened. What he noticed first was how poorly the room was furnished. There was only a trunk and a single bed, no rug, no pictures, no bedspread. What he noticed second was that it was only a room; there wasn't even a bathroom connected to it, and its emptiness stared out at him.

He ran through the downpour, over to the main house, and peered into the kitchen window. There she was, kneading dough on the counter. But it was only Estella; Jimmy wasn't in sight. He was about to tap the glass to get her attention when Mack walked into the kitchen, opened the refrigerator, and took out a bottle of beer. Estella turned to say something to him, and Mack laughed.

Nathan started to head back to the cottage. His shoes were so wet they were spongy. Water slid down his eyes, spilled off his hair, and into the neck of his shirt. There was no use in hurrying, he was completely soaked. He saw a light on in his mother's cottage. Find refuge there? He would leak buckets of water onto her floor. He looked at the way the wind tossed the tops of the trees, and, past his mother's cottage, he cut across the lawn. It was at that moment that lightning split the sky in half and the same winged creature he had seen on the pond swooped over the lawn and fell down. He started to run towards it, but his sneakers flopped off, and without stopping he ran out of them and through the pools of water on the grass. Jimmy was lying on the ground, her clothes stuck onto her skin. He thought she was dead, and feeling rage and panic, he called her name. But it was too noisy, his voice got swallowed. When he knelt down beside her, her face burst into a smile.

"I told them we needed rain. And it's raining. Isn't that amazing?"

"Yeah," he said, "but it's lightning, and you're out in the open."

"You're out in the open, too, and you're higher than me. And I have rubber soles on my sneakers, and you don't even have your sneakers on. You'd better lie down really flat. Come on, get rained on."

So he lay down next to her, and water pounded on his body till he turned flat and muddy. He wasn't even a boy anymore. Next to him, Jimmy wasn't even a girl. They were so wet, they were rivers of water. They were grass, they were ground, they were sky.

Dioxin Bagatelle

Colors get married and dance steps try
but a dance step is selfish. Diagrams
make dioxin look like a six-sided
dance with carbon prongs but dance steps
won't build up over time. Some of
the white leaks out, a strangeness

we can't recognize till marshes resemble
these rheumy stanzas but unchosen. Dioxin
likes breast milk. Daylight braids in equal
roses on both sides around people
fishing near Unocal in the battered
colors of secret Julys, colors dreamed

in the dreamathon before we sprayed
those brown-skinned people with our pink
so why was it called Agent
Orange in sixty-eight? State poppies try
to convert it to themselves but
there's some crossover. An interviewer asks

where a poem starts. He's disturbed
about the stanza. Its beauty
subverts intention. Little worlds are
images of big ones, crimes have
poets, a metaphor is meant to
self-destruct. Dioxin stays in a body

seven years, a lump forms in
the friendly tissue near her heart
like the last time she wants
to see someone's car. Lovers of
seafood, dockworkers, a swan named Myrtle
wade in Richmond's moat, the queen

is sick, her lord the chamberlain
is taking note, tearing up sentences
to make them clean. When they
danced, did they count or just
want to get out and drive
south, to be continually seen, seen?

Middle Ear

Say that moment crossing over isn't heard
Say the hammer-anvil-stirrup don't unfurl
Say the balance was upset

Say this balance was upset
Say the outside world doesn't ring

Say the mind's ear listening to an odd man singing
Say the moment crossing over starting somewhere out and in
Say the balance was upset

Say this balance was upset, and the singing falls faint
Say you turn yourself away from crowds of sound

Say the awed man singing sings to you

Say you don't know him. You don't.

And the balance is upset

Say the inside singing and the outside ringing and
    the moment crossing over breathing in
Say the whisper of the man sieves through
Say the moment crossing over is a stranger wisp

And the balance is upset
And the balance is upset

Say the moment crossing over rights the left
Say the moment crossing over is the ringing ear writing
Say the moment crossing over ends hear

Pure

for César Vallejo

To speak with a simple mouth.
No more
big words. Bread works.
Butter, a long walk
by the river works,
salt, fog, wood.

I know how to turn myself cold,
to cut everything off—
I can slice my heart to minnows,
but it's my wish
to remain alive, God with
and without me; those
who made me real to myself
have gone away and still

I would like to stay, the way he did,
though he was burning up
with longing and far
from home.
—He knew
he'd never see his home again
and he let that
purify him.

RICARDO PAU-LLOSA

Isla de Corcho

for René Touzet

Is music, then, a balcony
from which a shuffling of passings
is surmised, or is it
mortar and archway, or must it be
inkling, maestro, a suspicion
of survivals? We sit in rows
to watch ourselves listen
to your *danzas* and *contradanzas,*
the Cubanized European genres
which define a certain buoyancy
in our corky character. Cuba
promised us air and loyalty,
claimed it had the nerves
to shoot up to the surface,
swore it was a thing
lighter than its festive dangers.
The pearly throat of your keyboard is not
the ocean, despite the tight caress,
but it spells out possible horizons,
the ones we carry in the hidden pocket
of the invisible vest
upon the theoretical body
that stayed home while we fled.
Contradanza, from the English
country dance, seems to oppose
the *danza* in its Spanish emanation.
That is why language insists
we not trust it, look elsewhere
—to music, say, or to painting—
for the solid ambiguities,
the crest of feeling rising sharp
and foamless to overtake the calm view

of the horizon like a sovereign jaw.
The great lidless ear, amphitheatrical
conch. At its center, its stage,
the living vacuum where sound
sheds trembling theory to become
note upon chord upon phrase. Assembles
us. The melody returns from the cave
of child, from the unhinged door
of that rainy kiss, from any diffuse incident
whose molecules have mated by chance
to throw us into remembrance.
Listen, the tribe of sounds say,
for in the listening there is
a little mercy against the numb tide
and a sky too starry to guide us.
Close your eyes and listen.

Michael Who Walks by Night

For his sake drifting away from the true
windlessness, torn sails the aftermath
of him: white canvas suffering too vaguely
from the beautiful agreeing with these arguments,
but far away: sought him, found him

not, distant from image, archetype, the typical
sublime's encroachments, archaeology
of his innocence which is to be destroyed. Shaped,
shaping, shapes, and shape, the neverwhere
intact, the unearth disinterred. Hermes mi amor,

mi partida, mi pobreza: him my dark
of the moon, my mare nubium, oceanus
procellarum, whatever's not shown there, a man
who wants to make him shadowless. I windward
into disbelief unmoored, drowned

splendors of my own speech. Then beauty with his hooks
and pulleys, block and tackle has his way. Him
just across the boundary of the sayable, tradutore,
traditore, willingly acceding to any formulation
on the other side of words, spoken, spoken of,

but never said: him always
the him, object of the hymns I wrote, subject
to song, so he can't recognize himself, come down
to rescue his or mine, danger invites him, a popular
tune (taste of betrayal

on the humming tongue, the hearing ear,
but wrongly): my occupation or claim
on Argus-eyed blind night, trill, partial, whistling
untuned: this stubborn wind, his
mandolin. He knows I'd love.

Carvaggio Moderno

David with the Head of Goliath, 1609–10?

No bronze, paraphernalia, or feathers.
No euphoric cheers or parade. Simply
The slayer and his prey. The boy's body
Shines horrific as a candle. Without
Tenderness, the light cuts his skin
Across the arm; around a nipple; his chest
And neck; across the wrinkles of his brow,
His solemn and resilient lips: washed,
Still, unkissed. The light avails us down
To the youth's fist. From its clench, the giant's
Damaged walleyed head hangs unadored.

JENNIFER TONGE

Acrostic at Sarah's Request

Exalt me into flesh, each nerve feathering
at your right touch. Odd cannibal, incarnate me in you.
Touch what's made expressly to be touched, tap as on a sugar

maple, when I say *tongue,* I mean that quick conjunction of flesh
    and flame—*in*
excelsis—Deo, Deo,

Three Seaside Tales

The Man with the Spotted Dog

I was sitting at an outdoor café across from the ocean in Florida when I spotted the man with the spotted dog. I thought it was interesting. Me at a seaside resort and a man with a spotted dog. It reminded me of the famous story where a man meets a lady with a dog, also at a seaside resort, and has a long-term affair with her. A story noted for its pathos and irony, a particular combination of which characterizes the renowned author of the renowned story.

So. There I was in my short-shorts, gazing wearily at the spider veins in my legs, waiting for fate to intervene in my life. Thus I was melancholy, thinking of life's great themes—disintegration and death, loss and heartache—when the man with the spotted dog sat at the adjoining table and ordered a moccachino. The dog was small, but muscular and somewhat ill-tempered. It strained against its leash and yelped annoyingly. The man shook open his *New York Times* and ignored it. He wore navy-blue Nike shorts with an orange stripe and a Calvin Klein baseball cap. His sunglasses were chrome-plated Vuarnets. His legs were tanned and not too copiously hairy.

As I studied what parts of him were available around his newspaper, his dog barked angrily. At me, I suddenly realized. "Quiet!" I was gearing up to say to the dog, when the man folded his newspaper and addressed me. "Are you wearing perfume? The dog hates perfume."

I was wearing Ma Griffe by Carven. "Oh, I'm sorry. It's such an adorable dog," I lied.

"Come over here, so you won't have to shout," said the man.

That is how I first came to know the man and his dog. They were from Connecticut. It'd been a long time since I'd been to Connecticut. When I thought of Connecticut, I thought of the woods and pine needle floors and muddy streams with skinny, silver-colored minnows.

"You wouldn't know it anymore," said the man mournfully. "It's all urbanized and squalid."

That night we went on a date, and the dog came along. "I just can't leave him at the motel," said the man. I refrained from wearing Ma Griffe and prayed my underarm deodorant (slightly scented) would not set off the dog.

We went to a restaurant several blocks from the ocean where all the personnel wore lederhosen and Tyrolean hats. Our table had an absurd centerpiece which consisted of a rubber mermaid trapped in an oblong of frozen plastic, adorned with snakes and roses.

"That thing is really hideous," I said.

"Well, I wouldn't know. I try not to be critical." The man gave me a disdainful look. The dog licked my ankles and the tops of my shoes.

I decided to go out with the man for the following reasons: I happened to be in Florida visiting my elderly aunts, who were both nearly stone-deaf and lived in very small quarters at the Salt & Palm Condominium shouting at each other. I had been sleeping on the foldout sofa in the living room, and I felt as though I were always caught in their cross-fire. Also, Bessie and Fran were not cooks. For dinner we ate things like hard-boiled eggs and left-over Domino's pizza. I was in the mood for a real dinner. Also, the man was good-looking in a sulky sort of way. He had dark eyebrows that almost connected into one brow over the bridge of his nose. And his teeth were okay, very straight and white, no spaces. Other than those meager physical attributes, it's true he was not charming, even though he was obviously well-educated and liked animals (or so I deduced).

Now I was beginning to fear that, really, we had nothing in common and the dinner would be one long, painful drudgery, face to face, chewing and swallowing. The dog was extremely irritating, my ankle was beginning to chafe from the action of its tongue. The Bavarian-attired waitpeople were relentlessly cheerful in a bluff, overhearty, Germanic sort of way, and in a corner of the bar a group of customers had gathered to sing beer-hall songs. I hated everything about this place. The idea of bratwurst nauseated me. Spaetzle likewise.

"You're not a fan of the food? You should have said something."

The man, I now noticed, had an almost imperceptible smugness about his mouth, some small pursing of the lips with which he communicated his disapproval. I imagined him as a small child with a mother whose mouth he learned to imitate. I could picture him very clearly picking up his wretched little toys, making towers with his nasty little alphabet blocks. Even as a child, very clean. His lips beginning that prissy pursing. The more I imagined the man as a boy—screaming if his food items touched, washing his hands compulsively after riding a bus—the less likely it seemed he would ever own a dog, much less one who slobbered over my instep.

Now sprang to mind a picture of the man growing up in Connecticut near a big city in a white house with black shutters. His father, who had business internationally, was hardly ever at home. His mother, moody and removed, insisted upon certain standards of hygiene. I saw the boy, in impeccable slacks and shirt, standing forlornly on the sidelines while neighborhood kids tossed a football amongst themselves. A cast in one eye, he always appeared abstracted, inattentive. For this reason, teachers distrusted him, and one teacher went so far as to yank him brutally out of the cafeteria line and seat him in the cloakroom for twenty minutes. There among the damp smelling coats and galoshes of the day, he gazed out of a tiny, grimy window to a tiny, tremulous landscape. It seemed to represent his future: A sky with a moist cloud, a shaggy tree, and a dog with a few spots racing through.

O Chekhov! Where are you now? Because I want to wrap up this story of the man with the spotted dog, which is to say that I wanted the evening to be over. Perhaps I yearned to settle myself into the lumpy heft of the foldout sofa and listen to Bessie and Fran argue about laundry. But mostly I wanted the man on the other side of the trapped mermaid centerpiece to become kinder and more accessible and even funnier—to lean across the table and take my hand in his. "Darling," he would say, "I have been waiting for you always, and now it is our good fortune to meet at last."

Mary Ann

I f you see a colored person sitting on the bench in front of the Salt & Palm Condominium in Boca Raton, Florida, do not think she is a resident. No, she is working for somebody, waiting for her ride. She is probably a visiting nurse come to give someone an enema. Or a maid. At the front desk, Jacob buzzes in the visitors and others. Those he doesn't recognize, he telephones about. The carpet in the lobby is bright green with a band of paler green running up and down its angles, like a lawn, only more everlasting. There are stripes everywhere on the upholstery and a glass-topped coffee table in the shape of a swimming pool and a multitude of fake plants. Once in a while someone puts a real vase of flowers on the table, and this fools everyone who is used to the artificial. It is hard to tell what from what. I am very sleepy.

My employer is called Jim M——. I'm obliterating the last name in case he recognizes himself in this story I intend to publish and he decides to sue. Not that he is the type to sue. These people, as a rule, don't sue. Also, Mr. M——, who I do not mean to slander, has had a stroke and is very forgetful and disoriented, which is why I am here.

During the day I push him to the poolside in his wheelchair. His yellow sweater is around his shoulders, and on his head is a canvas hat with a plaid band. To me, he is very beautiful—small bones, tiny flat ears, his slacks always with a good crease, and nice shoes with white laces. His hair is silver and as thin as a halo and exceptionally well-behaved. As is Jim himself, a perfect gentleman, even though he is highly confused and does not always know which end is up. Poor Jim. In private I call him Jim.

"Penny for your thoughts," he said the other day. He stretched his trembly hand toward me, which was the signal for handholding. I am sure there are those who see us around the pool and feel—I am trying to imagine what they feel—disgusted.

Mrs. M——, who I always call Mrs. M——, is sometimes, I am sure, embarrassed by his behavior. "Give us a little kiss," he said the other day to the daughter of one of the residents. I had to laugh to myself because the daughter, who I will call Louise, took a backwards step and almost fell into the pool. She had dark hair twisted up and kept in place with a wooden spike. "That's a nice thing," I told her about the spike. Then she kissed him, and a look crossed her face. I know the feeling. His cheek like a moth, as if you were kissing something fluttering, about to fly apart. One good swat, and the pieces of Mr. M—— would turn to dust. I like my job.

Mrs. M—— is the opposite. She has a wedge-shaped body— skinny legs and an enormous torso. When she plunges into the water, she creates an enormous fan-shaped spray on either side of her top half, like the prow of a ship. She has a forceful voice and is of course much more practical than Mr. M——. You'd never catch Mrs. M—— smiling at a bird or throwing pebbles to a baby. You'd never catch her dribbling a little water on her pant leg just to watch the spot spread out. She does everything very fast— zip zip zip—she swims, she towels, she slaps on the Coppertone, she showers, she eats. She tells me, "Don't you think he needs a sweater today? It's a little chilly." Or "I was thinking he might like a ham sandwich and a pickle, and I'll have the same, thank you, dear." Mrs. M—— and I do not have conversations, and she never calls me by my name. In both these ways she's like my mother.

My mother who is not a maid and says she would never be a maid for any white people, God strike her dead. "Mama, I'm not a maid. I am a companion. A companion is different from a maid," I explain. "Idiot," she says. "Do you or do you not fix they's lunches?" "I may, on occasion, make a sandwich for two old people who can no longer do for themselves, yes, Mother." "Do you or do you not vacuum clean? Do you or do you not wash they's dishes?" My mother has eyes that could snap off the branch of a tree. "Answer me that."

This is what's true: When I go home at night, I am still in some part of my brain at the Salt & Palm sitting beside Jim and holding his hand or giving him sips of water from a paper cone or folding his yellow sweater and putting it on a shelf in his closet. I am still there with him in the living room on the gold sofa looking through the drapes with the parrot print at the waterway boats and the shimmery gray waves and the beautiful flower beds and lawns.

I know you are thinking the obvious, but it is not that simple. I do not want their *things*. What I would like is to be able to fall asleep in his California King with the lacy pillowcases—not for the purpose of luxury, but for the purpose of *understanding*. This is what you have to realize about me since this is the story of me, I am its central character, and Mr. and Mrs. M—— and all the folks around the pool and crossing and recrossing the green carpeting are subsidiary to me. Which is not the same in real life.

Here is my main point: The Salt & Palm Condominium, situated on a strip of land bordering the Gulf Stream Waterway in Boca Raton, Florida, is a sand-colored building whose insides duplicate the lawn and the hedges surrounding it. There are one-, two-, and three-bedroom units. Each has a balcony that overlooks the waterway and the harbor full of tall, drifting boats. The youngest inhabitants are in their sixties, and the oldest are pushing one hundred. Mostly retirees, though there are one or two well-preserved blond ladies who have jobs in the village. These are the questions which arise: What do the inhabitants of the Salt & Palm think about all day? And also: How is it that they take it all in stride? The boxy hedge and the gardeners who clip them, the poolside geraniums, the unwavering lawn, the waterway with its silver dazzles clucking around the little dock? The white plastic chaises, the grandchildren, the lunchtimes and dinnertimes, the clear pool always without bugs and twigs, the chrome railings gleaming like celestial bodies? And those other bodies with pedicures and hairdos and the lazy, ringed, freckled fingers reaching for the Bain de Soleil? And the slick, orange, hairless legs? Because I don't understand what these bodies contain other than themselves. As a student of creative writing, I am compelled to explore what baffles me. Oh, I am so tired, sometimes I wish I were dead.

To be truthful, I'm a little in love with Jim. Of all the bodies here, his is the most delicate and lovely. His skin is the color of glass. If you stand behind him at a certain time of day, you can see through the tip of his ear. Lord Jim, I call him, after one of those big schooners that comes into the waterway. When Louise heard me say it, she said, "Oh, Conrad," showing off. She and I have gotten friendly. "These people," she hisses—Louise hisses—"are total bigots. I just hope you realize that." She means well, but she is not a writer. She doesn't have the curiosity to put up with things. I try to explain about Mrs. M——'s nightgown, a full-length nightgown, pure white with pale blue satin bows on the lace straps and little tucks above a cluster of snowy pleats. I tell her that for me the nightgown—much too small for Mrs. M——now—is a symbol. "You're a romantic," Louise says.

At home my mother makes an apple pie. She is standing in her bra rolling out the crust. She swears a blue streak. She hates making pies. Now here is a person whose insides are full of crevices and whorls. Also, she is divorced. She's always reminded me of that tragic fact. "I am a divorced woman, Maryann, and in this world a single woman better know where she's at, or there'll be hell to pay to the piper." She is still mad at me for working at the Salt & Palm, even though it brings a good income. "Shit and damn," she says as she flops the crust into a glass dish. The kitchen light is grimy and dim due to the one bulb that's burned out in the overhead fixture. When she tried to repair it the other day, a little explosion followed by a shower of sparks occurred, so she said she better let sleeping dogs lie. I wanted to point out that there was nothing "sleeping" about a near electrocution, but these days she is so prickly with me, I did not dare. As a creative writing exercise, I take note of things as if for the first time: the row of metal canisters with dents on each of the lids, the lettering all faded on the SUGAR; a pile of laundry on a chair; shoes under the table since last week. Through our window with the dusty yellow valance, a depressing view of Mr. Oliphant's old, rusted Ford Falcon and our own clothesline with a green towel slapping in the wind. All this reminds me of the Salt & Palm and its calmness and beauty. I hear some kids screaming on their bicycles, and I cannot help but make a comparison.

My mother scratches under the strap of her bra. "Fuck and hell," she says, "I got to lose some of this poundage, or my underwear won't fit me." In figure she is not unlike Mrs. M——, though I have never seen, nor do I wish to see, Mrs. M—— in a bra.

Once the pie's in the oven, Mama looks me over. Her eyes are hot, and instinctively I flinch as if she would hit me, though she's never hit me. "What you looking at?" she says. "I know what you're thinking, don't think I don't." She looks around the room, and I see a small sadness crease her face before she marches out.

This is when I recall with shame what I did today when Mrs. M—— had gone shopping and Mr. M—— was taking his p.m.

nap. I went to the closet and removed the nightgown from its pink hanger. At first I only held it up to the window. It was so beautiful, the light poured into it and dazzled on the snowy pleats, the little tucks underneath the bodice. Then, I could not help it, I tried it on. In the full-length, I looked a way in which I'd never seen myself: as if the light had filled my body as well as the nightgown. You may think this is a vague metaphor, but it is the truth. I had become the light, and I had also become the nightgown. I myself: snowy, white, soft. I wish I could describe the feeling. At first I wanted to cry, and then I became dizzy. Luckily, I managed to take it off and neatly fold it and put it away before Mrs. M—— returned. Then I walked over to Jim, who was still napping, his head to one side on the pillow and drool coming out of the side of his lip. It crossed my mind I could kill him so easily. Just pick up a pillow and stuff it in his face. It wouldn't take hardly any strength.

I am looking out the window at the clothesline, and it's getting darker outside so that the green towel that flapped a few moments ago is a flapping silhouette that reminds me of a bat. I've always been good at description. Mr. Oliphant's old, rusty car is a medium-sized whale against the gray sky, and the one or two smudged stars which are trying to shine on our roof are like bottle caps at the bottom of a puddle. Of course I do not really want a nightgown such as the one I tried on this afternoon. What I want is the *feeling* of the nightgown. But, as I've already mentioned, it is hard to write down exactly what the feeling is. When I figure it out, I will insert it into this story, which I believe is drawing to a close.

The Phantom Ship

After a while, a white ship pulls into the waterway. Looming over everything—the palm trees and the swimming pool and the buildings that comprise the Salt & Palm Condominium—it reminds us of a whale. It intrudes into our peaceful scenario where we are sunbathing and reading our novels, filling us with awe and dread. It is so big, for one thing, and so close. If it were a different kind of vehicle, it would mow us down in our bikinis on our plastic chaises. It would flatten the hibiscus shrub and the sea grass and the little spider who makes her home in the deep nooks of the gardenia.

The sun moves behind a cloud, and now we can look up, up, as high as the top deck of the ship, as high as the row of portholes adjoining the top deck of the ship. No one. No one languishing over the railings, no one pining at the windows. This is, we decide, The Phantom Ship, driven by the waterway ghosts who are laughing invisibly on the top deck, throwing their heads back, and sipping cocktails out of blue stemmed glasses. They are still in their evening clothes. The one called Marie wears her hair in a chignon; she is leaning her black-stockinged leg against Charles, who appears lost in thought. "He is dreaming with his eyes open," says Priscilla, his mother. Other couples drift and float: a tall blond woman dances with a tall blond man. A burly fellow with a mustache storms by shaking his fist at Fred, the bellhop, who shivers in his red coat.

"Of what does Charles dream?" asks Marie, who is sad to be ignored by her handsome fiancé.

"He dreams always of a ship," says his mother, who knows him best.

"Always the same dream?"

The mother settles her enormous weight onto a deck chair, which creaks as she sits. "Yes. Always the same. I will tell it to you.

"A young man in search of his fortune sets sail on a lavish ocean liner. There he finds himself in the private stateroom of a beautiful woman and her companion, an older man with intensely blue eyes. There is a marble fireplace, a mantel adorned with yellow roses, wallpaper with a pattern of dense, green vines, a velvet chair, a silver tea service on a hammered brass table, an ottoman covered with silk monkeys, a Persian rug featuring stick figures scurrying up a ladder, a leather-bound volume of Heraclitus, and a cat. The cat sits on the woman's lap purring softly as she strokes it with a gloved hand. Her companion paces in front of the fire, which shoots up its blazing pinnacles behind him, crackling and hissing, as if parodying the man's restless mood. The window is a dark square framed by a shimmering drapery. 'Oh wonder of wonders,' the woman is saying, 'I wonder where I left my handkerchief?'

"The woman and the man proceed to talk to each other in low voices, too muted for the dreamer to hear. It is as if he were invisible to them, as they are inaudible to him, as if a thick transparent substance separates the dreamer from the dream. It occurs to him to test this theory by snatching the cat from the woman's lap. As he predicted, he is unable to do so—his hand encounters something implacable which holds it in check. Thus he sprawls on the rug and contents himself with studying the woman—her lovely brown eyes, the paleness of her skin, her hair which is auburn and curled. She is familiar to him, the way her hands stroke the cat, even the rings on her fingers—he feels as if he's seen them before when he was much younger, perhaps in a dream.

"He is startled by a movement in the dense vines of the wallpaper behind her head. A little man, no more than two inches long, is crawling along, hoisting his tiny body up and over the tangle of spindly vines, balancing himself now and then on the wide palettes of the leaves. He is on his way to rescue his wife, who is trapped under the spider who has made her home in the deep nooks of the gardenia. On and on he climbs, the faint cries of his wife peppering the distance between them. Just then there is a terrible noise which brings the dreamer back to himself. The woman stroking the cat has just shot the man pacing in front of the fireplace. She sits with a puzzled look on her face, staring at the tip of the smoking revolver. 'What should I do now?' she asks the dreamer. She looks so helpless, vulnerable. He wracks his mind for some comforting words to say to her, but just then he wakes up."

"Always at the same point?" asks Marie, fingering the moire of Charles's cuff.

"Always," says Priscilla his mother, smiling fondly at her son, who at this moment is snapping into an elated consciousness. "Marie!" he says, kissing his fiancée passionately.

Overhead, a jet soars, and the sides of the enormous phantom ship tremble and dip.

And the little wife, will she be saved? Will her valiant husband continue to swing and climb toward her? From here, her cries pepper the distance like the cries of a cricket or the chattering of ice cubes. Our fingers mark the page in our novel, which begins: "He spoke no more, but after a pause softly groped his way out of the room..." So, too, the phantom ship gropes softly down the waterway. Where to? Who knows?

Girl in a Library

...But my mind, gone out in tenderness,
Shrinks from its object...
              —Randall Jarrell

I want to find my way back to her,
to help her, to grab her hand, pull her
up from the wooden floor of the stacks
where she's reading accounts of the hatchet
murders of Lizzie Borden's harsh parents
as if she could learn something about
life if she knew all the cuts and slashes;

her essay on Wordsworth or Keats
only a knot in her belly, a faint pressure
at her temples. She's pale, it's five years
before the first migraine, but the dreamy
flush has already drained from her face.
I want to lead her out of the library,
to sit with her on a bench under a still

living elm tree, be *one who understands*,
but even today I don't understand,
I want to shake her and want to assure her,
to hold her—but love's not safe for her,
although she craves what she knows
of it, love's a snare, a closed door,
a dank cell. Maybe she should just leave

the campus, take a train to Fall River,
inspect Lizzie's room, the rigid corsets
and buttoned shoes, the horsehair sofas,
the kitchen's rank stew. Hell. Bleak
loyal judgmental journals of a next-door

neighbor—not a friend, Lizzie had no friend.
If only she could follow one trajectory

of thought, a plan, invent a journey
out of this place, a vocation—
but without me to guide her, where
would she go? And what did I ever offer,
what stiffening of spine? What goal?
Rather, stiffening of soul, her soul
cocooned in the library's trivia.

Soul circling its lessons. What can I say
before she walks like a ghost in white lace
carrying her bouquet of stephanotis,
her father beaming innocently at her side,
a boy waiting, trembling, to shape her?
He's innocent, too, we are all innocent,
even Lizzie Borden who surely did take

the axe. It was so hot that summer morning.
The hardhearted stepmother, heavy hand
of the father. There was another daughter
they favored, and Lizzie, stewing at home,
heavy smell of mutton in the pores
of history. But this girl, her story's
still a mystery—I tell myself she's a quick

study, a survivor. There's still time.
Soon she'll close the bloody book,
slink past the lit carrels, through
the library's heavy door to the world.
Is it too late to try to touch her,
kneel beside her on the dusty floor
where we're avoiding her assignment?

The Tenants

I saw them everywhere: in the backyard
spiraling up inside the pale lilacs, invisible

in the hall closet where old books were stored,
even playing in the fireplace ash. Late at night,

I'd bump into them in the bathroom. The tile floor
was icy and they were on their knees, all those

homeless spirits, blowing night air into a cold fog.
They watched me learn to dance over that floor,

my feet turning blue as a fresh bruise. Oh, they
were in the basement, too, snoozing and snoring,

exhaling clouds of oil fumes and dirt from every duct.
Mostly, I heard them laugh. Very late, after everyone was in bed,

they sailed into my room telling me *roll over.*
But they were restless, climbing out the window

and ruining the ivy if I so much as blinked twice.
Leave, I'd say, but they'd look limp and listless, even

a bit damp and I'd say *never mind.* They were most comfortable
in candlelight, safe in the dining room where my mother

set places for them each night when the dark outside
matched the darkness inside. She created a feast

of letters and numbers, the words *yes* and *no.*
How they loved to sip from the highball glass she tilted

upside down, how they hurried to fill up that glass! We watched
their giddy spins over the tabletop forming chains of letters

and words. My mother asked them so many questions,
like *why not move in?* Little droplets shivered over the table

and they lapped it all up. Once invited, they never left.
They kept me up all night with silent chatter, like visiting

children who don't know when *dinner in five minutes*
really means *go home.* They thrust tiny fingers

down the neck of my pajamas, accused me of hogging
the covers, spoke all night of *secret messages.*

Bored, they stooped to stealing car keys then
cash, gossiping about our careless fumblings,

never minding that I was listening,
that I heard it all.

Triclinuim: Couple Bending
to a Burning Photo

Inside ourselves,
inside ourselves so long
    we are engravened there. Inside
the hot streets mazing
    from the Suq to fractious

cul-de-sacs, piss smell
  & whitewashed alleyways,
    mules & taxi radios throbbing Rai
    & still inside ourselves.
(Still with our own canopic jar—
  pulsing from its negative

    the sonogram, the inkstain heart:
pinprick size & lifesize both.
    Bitter the book.
  Bitter like vinegar
    the unwritten book.)

Boys with head lice tug our sleeves
  & when with a trowel
    does the site grow laden,
    teetering up & sealed
at last by brick?
  Suddenly the dicey neighborhood,

    Kom al-Shogafa, gives way.
Ticket booth, a caftaned watchman
    sipping tea,
a single olive tree—off-season
    it is permitted

to descend alone. Down
    the creaking ladder like Aeneas
        & we test each trembling rung,
            all to ourselves the shaft,
the fetid water ankle-deep,
    the walls this far below the June sun

        cool to the touch in the edgelight
of twenty-watt bulbs,
        strung along the switchbacking galleries,
room after catacomb room.
        & still inside ourselves.

By rope the dead were pulleyed
    down the shaft, slow plummet
        of urn, sarcophagi groaning
            to rest in stuccoed niches—
Thoth & Isis Hermes Christ,
    fish & falcon eye

        blinking open to our flashlight,
Anubus in bas relief
        in armor of a Roman legionnaire.
    A confusion of styles
        and religious tradition.

Capital with sacred bull,
    seated water-streaked baboon,
        room upon room
        inside ourselves,
Caduceus seething blue vipers.
    Dead end & gallery & on her knees

        N. peers haloed in the bulb's
burnished shimmer, stroking cool stone,
        a niche for a child,
    barely the length of her arm.
        & now before us the famed

vaulted room, dome soaring up
   as the lights begin to flicker,
      blinking twice & off.
         Darkness so thick we breathe it.
Then N. with flashlight
   rummaging her backpack

     for the grapes & cheese,
baguette & tannic
     Sinai merlot
("Omar Khayam Red"),
       her jackknife glinting in the beam.

All this way. All this way
   to mourn again our child in a room
      of couches hewn from living rock.
     Triclinuim—
"the place of banquet
   for remembrance of the dead."

   Far-off drip of cistern water
& to the stone we pour
     the first libation,
   the black wine hissing out.
       O spirit beyond hunger,

we set down to you such offerings
   as will appease thee, body
     unborn of our bodies,
       bread of our bread.
O circle within circle, imprinted gray

    on the sonogram's firmament,
crosses & arrows glyphed
     across thee to map thy size.
We strike the lighter & we lay your photo
      on the ancient threshing floor of souls

& only for an instant do you flare.

Analysis of the Rose as Sentimental Despair

Cy Twombley, set of five paintings, 1985

Here it is, the Impressionist garden
raised to another level of fluidity,
no shape assembling itself
in a wash of pink and red,

a watery garden where one color flows
into another, roses blazing and bleeding,
pink, crimson, carmine, scarlet,
until the color flames to blood,

the colours from his own heart,
and the heart, too, blazes and breaks
open, beauty giving way
to death, the eternal

in the ephemeral. No, not giving way
exactly, it's embedded in the bud, the vein.
Rose, oh sheer contradiction—
what made the poets weep whose words fly

like flags above the paintings.
Those early-waking grievers—Rumi,
Rilke, Leopardi—oh, how each of them loved his sadness.
. . . his pains are delectable, his flames are like water.

They were bereft without their pain.
And I am thinking now
of the women they could never quite love
(loving the Idea, but not the Thing itself),

loving the memory of rose petals
strewn across a bed, but not
the rumpled, semen-stained sheets.
I am thinking of Clara Westhoff

to Paula Becker: "I am so very housebound...
a house that has to be built—and built
and built—and the whole world
stands there around me. And it will not let me go."

And I am also thinking
of my friend Larry Levis, a poet
who loved Rilke, who wrapped himself
in his despair, the way he might have

worn an old quilt all through
one Thanksgiving in Iowa City
when the heat didn't work. It would have
warmed and comforted him. That was long ago,

before betrayal, divorce, all the old
home remedies for pain—Marcia and Larry
were still together then, and I remember
envying them that. I don't remember

what we ate or what we talked about,
all three of us poets—poetry, probably,
instead of love—but I remember
the black lakes of his eyes, the eyes

of an old man even then,
though he was my age, not even forty,
the way he touched his mustache
and laughed ruefully at his own bad jokes.

I don't know what had wounded him.
About grief he was "enthusiastic, but wrong,"
as he said of his students' poems.
When we laughed, our breath

drew clouds in the air
above the rented dining room table.
But here, in these paintings, the clouds
are roses, clouds of them drifting

and spilling over in the rain, a lake
of roses, roses streaked with rain,
so many of them you can't tell
one from another. If to know beauty is to live

with loss, then why should we love
our grief so much? It's nothing special.
And if death is the extinguishing of all form,
as the painter sees, it is also the rose made new

again and again, as he also sees,
the way I once stood, lost
in my sorrow, in the shallows
of Deer Lake. Above me, the live oaks

reached out their arms the way a mother
might open her arms for her child
to step inside, then Cosmo barked and ran
back and forth across the narrow dam,

until he slipped and fell and came up
swimming. He had a look of such surprise
that he could stay afloat! And then
I raised my face to the place where the sun

stole through the dense heaven of leaves,
and for a moment—just once, though it was enough—
I was somewhere else, I was a body
composed almost wholly of light.

And Larry? Years later, he died.
His heart just blazed and burst
open. It was spring, maybe roses bloomed
beside the back steps of his house in Virginia.

It was days before anyone found him, his face
already beginning to disappear, like a drawing
slowly being erased around the edges.
Most of the time he'd been troubled,

I don't know why exactly—the lovelorn
vineyards of California? the poverty
of horses?—for no reason and many reasons,
maybe, and maybe just because he was himself,

a man who courted his despair, shyly,
tenderly, the way he courted women,
but he was sober, writing again,
and after he died his friend took the poems

and made a book of elegies, as all poems are,
a book I am holding right now. Once,
when he was young, he wrote a poem
set on the morning after his death.

My body is a white thing . . . now,
he wrote. *. . . and there is nothing left but these flies,*
polished and swarming frankly in the sun.

What did his sorrow ever do for him?
It couldn't save him, any more than love could.
But that's not the point. What *is* the point?
To know death, to breathe deeply

of its aroma, to hold it close to the heart
as one might hold a rose, and still desire
to go on living, that is the human,
the remarkable thing. For a long time, he did.

Now he is water, rose petals
in an Impressionist garden, these rose petals
dashed to the ground, drifting and blowing
in the late spring rain.

for Larry Levis (1946–1996)

JEREDITH MERRIN

Norway Maple, Cut Down

November 1997

Its bare branches the winter before
were exuberant scrawls
against a blank sky about
to snow and then snowing,
or runes punctuated
by the brownish-gray
question marks of squirrels.
And this fall, the leaves
were so gold they looked heavy
as Cleopatra's burnished throne
or as some feeling unexpressed.
The one tree in the yard,
casting lace on the concrete stoop,
blocking an alleyway from view.

Our garrulous German landlady,
a Transylvanian postwar
émigré, with no explanation or
warning ordered the forty-foot
healthy tree cut down.
Inhabiting a squat, brick house
behind oversized security lights,
two doors from our half-double
on a pretty Victorian street,
she'd worked years and years
in department stores, putting away
nickels and dollars for property—
more money, more property.

One more incidence of
a small or large brutality
and there's nothing you can do:

the salacious welfare worker
in charge of your case;
the ash blonde in expensive shoes
who enjoys spoiling another
woman's self-esteem with a sneer;
any of the perennial
bullies of history, who
always could line up your family
and shoot them in a ditch.

Why didn't she relent,
when on that morning—the man
waiting, tethered up in the tree—
we pleaded with her, offering
to pay the workman's fee,
and surprising ourselves with tears?
Was she trying to please (or in a way
to *be*) her father, long dead,
a farmer in the Old Country she
talked and talked about, and who had
once, she said, cut down an entire
orchard of apricot trees?

Was she prodded by a kind of envy?
Married and divorced young,
she'd never remarried;
and one time, inspecting
the apartment we'd furnished
—my partner and I, living openly
together—she startled us,
blurting, "*I* could live with a woman.
But I have bad luck. Probably,
she not work hard, like me."
Busy, self-assigned patroller
of the street—had age made her
terrified of the free-falling leaves
she complained about:
"A mess! A big mess!"?

Determined, she stood mid-yard:
white-haired, blue-eyed, seventy-eight
and stocky, in her thriftshop
motley of flowers and stripes.
Among the bagged and unbagged
leaves that I'd just raked,
she shouted, "This is not your
property, this is *my* property.
You want a tree, move out!
Move to a farm if you want
trees!" Then, "Do it!"
to the dangling man, awaiting
his order; "I pay you. Just do it!"
It took hours, it took all day.

Leaning back in a patio chair
June afternoons, you could see
three or four layered greens
juxtaposed with blue puzzle pieces
carved by the five-lobed shapes.
Indoors, every season,
on the bone-white walls
that renters live with,
patterns of light and shade
altered as the tree altered,
like slightly rearranged
but lifelong compulsions,
and like the always available
possibility of changing your mind.

GRAY JACOBIK

The Ideal

As if their very comeliness were centrifugal,
one falls forward slightly toward
the husband and wife standing together
under the outdoor lights of a summer party.
Sunburnt, vibrant, expressive, perfectly
proportioned, they make clear, unwittingly
and in relief, our ordinary, passably-attractive selves.
God and goddess, or king and queen, amassing
mythic energy as they speak and gesture,
they are sweet-tempered and thoughtful,
so the sentiment that they exist to diminishing
the rest of us quickly shows itself as jealousy.
One expects tragedy to befall them, although,
one hopes, all the same, tragedy will be
continually forestalled, for who could wish
perfection marred? What is it to stand among
the less well-formed, the simply plain with
too short or too long noses, jutting or receding
chins and all the other oddments of contour
and bulk that are the common human lot?
Perhaps they see themselves as less attractive
than they are, know one another's frailties,
foibles, late-night fears, and yet these forms
of model grace—body, face—must astound
and beguile each as they beguile us who relive,
sadly, standing before them, self-conscious
in the light, the long-buried dream we clung to
in our youth: one day we, too, would be beautiful.

REETIKA VAZIRANI

Going to See the Taj Mahal

1959

When we set out on the train to Agra
I thought, What an old palace we are going to see,
    it's an old grave.
I was tired when we reached the station and you hired a taxi
to take us to the steps of the Taj Mahal;
you couldn't even wait until morning,
said it was something to take in by moonlight,
white marble against black sky is a great sight in moonlight
    you said
(marble just cleaned for a holiday).
And there beyond our driver's wheel I saw the domes—
the large dome and the four surrounding domes.
The silhouette stood out so clearly that for a moment
I forgot this fact in the midst of the splendor
(the long stretch of grass leading up to the site):
the Empress Mumtaz, she bore fourteen heirs for Shah Jahan—
absurd to forget Mumtaz at her marble grave,
marble banded with prophecy and verse.

But what did I know of the Empress except this tomb?
So I pictured her this way:
she was not a beauty, nor especially devout
(always slow to cover her head).
On Thursdays when the open market came past the red
    stone quarry,
she dressed as her handmaid
and took a poor cloth sack into town
where she bartered for beads women wore on ordinary days;
and secretly with cheap dyes she'd paint herself into the wild
    casual beauty of youth
(the kohl inexpertly applied but alluring).
Then she gave her sack away or left it on the road

should someone find it hoarded in her suite—
the Empress buying this five-and-dime garbage!
And she imagined her life without the constant royal curfew.
There were places she couldn't go—there were even daily
     attractions at the well,
attractions too scandalous to list.

If only the Emperor's architects knew her!—
to free them from the illusions which inspired the tomb,
to free them from the wished-for glamour of a Mumtaz.

How Aliens Think

Green is the color that defines them, of course. They don't realize yet, but it's already there in the picture.

Look closely, and Susan's wearing a grass-green peridot and pearl ring on her engagement finger, for Jim, who's coming to meet her as the *S.S. Carinthia* steams into New York Harbor. And Keith has on his olive-checked shirt while they stand with their Fulbright group at the lower-deck rail, catching the last of the sea breeze and watching for Manhattan to appear out of the whitening August haze.

Finally here she is, unbelievable but true: New York materializing lightly over the ruffled water. The crystalline formation rises in outline, higher and higher: a pure sci-fi dream of a city.

—*The door dilated,* Keith declaims, making a kind of spaceman salute.

Susan has both hands tight on the rail. —So, we actually did it, we left—

These are not the oppressed aliens that Emma Lazarus expected, the huddled masses yearning. They're something else, "accidentals," an ornithologist would call them. In 1962, it's not yet the big wave of Eurotrash—just educated drifters blown off current by some personal disaffection.

Keith and Susan are headed for the same New England university, and have made a convenient alliance. She's confessed to him, somewhere out there on the gray Atlantic, her evil habit of poaching married men, which, she insists, *is now over*! Hence the plan for Jim to get a Mexican divorce, and for the two of them to reunite forever after this year, in Texas, where he has a legitimate job. Keith has described to her his mad efforts to get a queer life among his native Yorkshire dales, despite the family's prominence in their banker's villa, despite a rural world in which bestiality is the only known perversion, and despite the wide-open moorland, its low stone walls and general lack of cover. *For miles and miles about, there's ne'er a bush,* he quotes bitterly—how true that is!

Even at Cambridge, in all other ways a paradise, Keith felt constrained by his parents' expectations for their only son. Their presence stuck in his head so obstinately, the only hope he had was to leave the country.

Now Manhattan's closer, threatening to become something real, made of steel-reinforced concrete as well as glass.

—Never mind, Keith says. —Look, we already *know* the language—how hard can it be?

—Right, says Susan. —Exactly my sentiments.

Carinthia docks on the lordly Hudson side. When they've run the Customs gauntlet, distant relatives of Keith claim him for the two weeks until college starts. No sign of Jim, though, anywhere. Susan sets to and hauls her suitcase to the taxi rank. At least she has the name of his hotel.

But, good Christ! Manhattan at ground level is one continuing assault of explosive noise and motion—insane jackhammers going at you from this side, backhoes clawing and grinding in the lot across the street, sirens in perpetual spasm. And this huge fist of heat clamps down on her—ninety-five degrees registered on a display. A news billboard says this marks a third summer of record drought and temperatures. The street simmers with radiated fire. Susan has no hat, no sunglasses. Nobody ever *told* her about this. In the bag clenched against her ribs she has just sixty dollars. She waits in line half an hour for a cab: time enough to suspect an irreparable mistake. Those three years' worth of absolute belief that she and Jim were each other's great love and best friend, her confidence that they would really end up together—some unknown percentage of all that is being sweated out of her, secretly evaporated away, every minute while she's standing on this yellow line.

She does find Jim, in the cool hotel lounge, convinced of course that this was their original agreement. Susan lets it pass, why not? Their room is wonderfully high up, with a view on some avenue, a shower to experiment with, and a bed for making wonderfully clean, air-conditioned love. Everything's fine again, America looking better by the minute.

Next day, Jim takes her along to an expensive lunch with the editor who's bringing out his study of Ezra Pound and Propertius. A cheerful guy, he orders an extra-fine bottle of wine; and what he really wants to do, it appears, is tell them his story of how William Empson, in Hong Kong before the war, arranged for Mrs. Empson to give him his first fuck, even leading him by hand to the marital bed itself.

A good fuck, was it? He confides, smugly, that it was an incomparable educational experience.

Another day, and Jim is leaving, authentic Green Card in his wallet, for the flight to Texas. Susan begs thirty dollars off him: taking money feels like a dirty thing to do, but she needs the cash. But then, the goodbye kiss she gives him feels dirty, too—the first time it's ever felt that way. Shaken, as if by one more bad omen, she goes back into the hotel lobby and calls a number written on a postcard: Lili's, on East 11th.

An Australian friend made the connection for her, Ed the philosopher, who was a member along with Lili and Germaine Greer of the Sydney Push—a group formed around the libertarian thinker John Anderson, and now scattered worldwide. Lili has since become a journalist, entertainment correspondent in the U.S. for a Sydney paper. Susan holds the battered postcard that Ed passed on to her. Sure, it says, in letters blurred by sweaty contact, August is her slow season. Ed's bloody Pom is welcome to stay.

The cab lets Susan off in front of a row of brick tenements hung with black fire escapes. There's a corner shop with fruit displayed, and she buys six peaches. Under the eleven o'clock blaze of sun, her too-thick shirt and jeans cling like wet armor on her skin. In the minutes it takes to drag her stuff to the right door and press the button, she's panting like a dog. Then, the sound of flip-flops on the staircase, and Lili, in a muumuu with a pattern of emerald leaves, leads the way upstairs into a room where fans chatter in the windows.

Susan does a visual check, and figures this is just a one-room flat. Another moment of awful doubt: what's she let herself in for now?

—*Christ*, girl, you look *fucked*! Lili says. She reaches into the fridge for a bottle of cold bubbly water, pours a glass, and puts it into Susan's hand. —Take this for a start.

The cooling liquid goes down, percolating through membranes into millions of grateful cells. And Susan's becoming vaguely conscious of her enormous luck, here, falling into the hands of a true guide and psychopomp. Because Lili, who is technically almost her own age, has lived like a bubble on the flood from the day she was born, the child of Jewish refugees surviving the war, somehow, in Italy. She escaped the DP camps with her parents to Australia, and has escaped again to New York, where she's in love with the city forever. Lili owns all the keys. She knows, she always knew, how to be an alien.

The apartment is quickly decoded: Lili sleeps in the curtained alcove to the right of the door, and to the left are the fridge, stove, sink, and a hip-bath fitted ingeniously under the lift-up countertop. The toilet, down the corridor, is shared with other tenants—it's unspeakable, what can you do?—and you take the toilet roll in with you and bring it back after. About the guest bed, ready made up under the window there: it's a good idea to tap on it several times, up and down, before getting in. That's to allow the roaches time to move out; if you pull the sheet back too suddenly, you might not like what you see. (Out of curiosity, Susan tries just that a few nights later, and a dozen roaches dash about hysterically. She feels so embarrassed for them.)

—Y'see, Lili explains, —even if ya bomb the bastards, which I do once in a while, the neighbors bomb them right back.

So this is downtown America. Susan's never lived in such a density of vermin before, with roaches into everything but the freezer, rats patrolling the alley at night, and a late-summer praying mantis living in the window box of herbs behind the sink. But she's never met, either, anyone like Lili, who makes this generous sacrifice without question, letting an absolute stranger come in to share her space. If she'd known, she'd never have dared ask. Even trying to say thanks, she stammers.

—So, Lili says, grinning, —your bloke's buggered off to Texas, eh? Typical! What d'*you* think of that?

—Well, it was the deal he got. See, I'm buggering off to Boston for a year, that's *my* deal, while he works out this divorce. Meanwhile I've only seventy-five dollars to last two weeks. And here's all I brought you: six peaches.

This stirs Lili's pride: she can deliver New York for that much, and give change back.

That afternoon they hit 14th Street and the sale at Gimbels, where Susan gets a loose, dark-red shirtdress, cut above the knee, for seven-fifty. Green sunglasses off the street: two-fifty. Later, with Susan wearing her new *schmatte,* they take a sunset walk past Delancey Street to the East River view. Next day to Blooming-dale's, just to check out the top-price stuff for fall—and there by pure chance is Lili's friend Jeannie, the model with a spread in this month's *Vogue,* going through the racks.

Jeannie invites them into her dressing room while she tries on a couple of things. She strips down to a tiny black bra and bikini briefs, shakes out her dark hair, and coolly turns herself before the mirrors. Susan has never seen a world-class beauty up close before, and almost naked. The symmetrical line of Jeannie's body seems as if newly drawn, in one long stroke of some divine sty-lus—finished off with a horizontal comma at the navel. No won-der Jeannie doesn't mind them looking: she's astonishing from any angle.

—My God, the flab! she moans, stroking her pale-tan midriff.
—I have to starve *five pounds* off, by September.
—Such a bitch, says Lili. —As if we weren't dying of envy already.

Jeannie laughs, and zips something on, smoothing and turning, looking at herself over her shoulder, then unzips, throws it down, and starts over. This is a lousy year, in her view—the colors are all muddy—nothing looks good except jeans anymore.

Lili takes leave with a kiss, and says hi to a young man sitting alone, sulking on a bench outside.

—That's Jeannie's boyfriend—French, she tells Susan.
—Almost as pretty as her. And awfully young, isn't he?
—I should bloody hope so! She's put in her time, y'know, with those rich old buggers when she was nineteen, twenty. Now she can afford to please herself—it's fair enough.

The next day, they ride the Staten Island ferry for a nickel, then it's to Ratner's for blintzes. At the weekend, they do Jones Beach, then a cocktail party in a fiftieth-floor apartment somewhere in Midtown. A thunderstorm has just passed through when they arrive, leaving tattered veils of cloud drifting past the huge win-dows, changing slowly from gray to lavender. Everything inside the apartment is in pale-neutral, and the women wear black dresses, except Lili in her leopard-print drape, and Susan in the red shift that she takes off only for sleep, or to wash.

Then they're in a group talking. Susan edges herself to where she can look out and watch the Chrysler building glow in the dimming light. Someone brings up the Royal Family, right in her face, so she answers, automatically: —Oh, sod the frigging royals, bloodsuckers, who gives a shit?

Which an older fellow, whom Lili introduced as Manny, takes as a come-on. He attaches himself to her, bringing her refills of gin and tonic, tells her he's in the theater business, and spins her a long joke about a little Jewish guy who makes money and goes to London for a bespoke suit, then stands in front of the tailor's mirror, draws himself up, and utters these words: *Pity we lost India!*

And Susan just does not get it. What is so damn funny—why is Manny bent over with tears of laughter in his eyes? He repeats the punchline, shaking with the hilarity of it. She understands the words, sure, *Pity we lost India,* but what the fuck is the *point*? Nobody Susan knows, or can even imagine knowing in her New Left circle, would be capable of thinking about India's independence that way. She's beginning to worry about aspects of the language here that she doesn't grasp: traps under the apparent familiarity.

But Manny's not done with her yet. He gets serious: —You could make it here, kid, y'know that? With that mouth on ya, and the accent? No, listen, I'm telling ya the truth! Ya gotta fix the hair—I can recommend a guy. And those eyebrows! Gotta lose the sad-clown look, know what I mean? Do the eyebrows right, it makes all the difference. Believe me. 'Cause I think you got a lot going for you, so make the most of yourself. Know what I mean?

Well, she appreciates his advice, yes, she does. Will seriously think it over. (For this, too, is America, land of perfectibility.)

Then Lili pulls her away—they have to go, catch a ride right now: —Just forget all that. Manny doesn't know shit about you, remember? We're going down to the Village for pizza—Glen and Rob have a car.

—Guys in the black leather?

—Sure, they're fine. They're both social workers—you never have to worry about fucking 'em, the whores give 'em free blow jobs all the time.

—I see.

Silent memo to herself: ask Lili privately what the blow job is.

It's related, conceivably, to the graffiti she's noticed on the local subway platform: *George sucks*. Which suggests some version of the old-style *soixante-neuf*? Well, best to be sure.

They park in Greenwich Village, and walk a few blocks to John's Pizza. But before they arrive, Susan catches a vision across an intersection that stops her cold. It is some kind of superhuman, well over six feet, and the dark-bronze face and those bare, polished biceps announce him as a black man—but he's wearing a woman's outfit that puts Lili's flamboyance to shame. A fuchsia boa winds loosely about the shoulders, shining bangles and charms hang from the neck and wrists, and that drop-dead dress is made in alternating panels of black and vivid aquamarine satin, with a short flip skirt. The final touch, a great floppy beret, blue and black check. He turns and paces aloofly along opposite them, showing off gold high-heels and black fishnets, and Jeannie herself couldn't command a more sinuous walk.

—Who is *that*? Susan asks.

Glen answers. —Who, Marlene? She's here every weekend, it's her beat.

His indifferent tone tells much. There are aliens and non-aliens, and evidently Marlene is at home in this place, whether Glen likes it or not. But how would Keith, she wonders, himself a village boy, take this revelation?

The day before Susan leaves on the train for Boston, Lili prepares for a flight to Hollywood, where Liz Taylor and Richard Burton have scheduled a press reception. Susan's vastly impressed that Lili will meet Burton, since she remembers his performance as Coriolanus at the Old Vic, before he was a film star: that voice with its ominous resonance, and the great silences even more.

—Darlin', listen to me, Lili says, and the flat edge of her accent cuts memory down to size. —You and me don't give a fuck about Liz 'n' Richard. Listen. *These are not real people.* What this is, is a *press conference*, and maybe they'll show up, maybe not. It's just my job.

Even so, Lili spends Labor Day Monday applying beauty treatments handed down by her grandmother, in case Hollywood does show up. She whisks together a mask of yogurt, cucumber, and honey for the face; then an egg and lemon mix to massage into her hair. After her bath, she rests with cold herbal tea bags laid on her eyelids. By the evening, Lili's skin shines gold, with an under-tint of olive; her gray eyes resemble smoky moonstones, and her blond hair, cut straight at the jawline, swings free like shaken silk.

Susan says it candidly: she's beautiful.

—Just the job, darlin'. Do what I can, given the limitations.

Lili gestures towards her body—short, strong, and rounded, on the Slavic model (when she goes out at night, she disciplines it with a ferocious Playtex panty-girdle). But her hands are small and exquisitely kept: and deny it as she would, she cares about that.

Susan thinks she'll remember everything about her time with Lili, but she doesn't remember the morning she left—only that the summer weather has broken, and rain is hammering the city as she catches the train north. It's understood, though, that Lili never leaves New York, except on business or for her mother in Sydney. If Susan is to stay connected, it's up to her.

Keith and Susan meet again at the International Student Center reception, over platters of bland cheese cubes ringed with Ritz crackers and grapes. They recognize not just each other, but a shared mood of dreamy loss, which it turns out has the same source: they've each caught a glimpse of Greenwich Village, and lost it again. *The Village,* which is shorthand for everything: the street life, espresso bars on the corner, jazz clubs, invisible airs of incense and grass fumes rising from dim groups among the Washington Square tree-lined alleys, and then, the entertainers under the arch...

—And then, Keith tells her in awed secrecy, —there was this *extraordinary* black man on the street, some gorgeous Watusi in a red tam-o'-shanter and a *miniskirt,* no less.

—Of course—I saw him. Six foot five, in full makeup and heels, yes!

—Oh my God, wasn't he amazing?

—Except that the one I saw had on a blue and black tam, dress to match.

—Is it possible there's *two* super-tall transvestites out there?

—Anything's possible, Susan says, admitting her submission as true Village believer. —A guy I was with said her name was Mar-lene.

—You were introduced?

—No, no—it's what he said.

—So where were you staying?

—East 11th. Bit of a dump, frankly. Every morning around six, incredible traffic noise and everything started up. Still, you could even *walk* to the Village.

—You and Jim?

—No, no, he left. I stayed with Lili, this journalist I sort of knew.

Susan's bragging; she knows it and can't help herself, with Keith eating it up.

—I was stuck way out in Westchester, he says, grimacing. —Imagine High Wycombe, only the houses and everything inflated to double-size.

The two of them seal their bond through a disparagement of Boston and surroundings.

—Problem is, says Keith, —everything round here's so hopelessly déjà vu. Sort of like Manchester but with a river.

—Exactly. And all these other areas looking like bloody *Neasden,* only the houses are made of tarpaper and wood.

—Exactly. Susan, I should tell you, I've made a promise to myself. Keith looks off into the far reaches of the cafeteria, over his Jell-O and hermit with faux cream on the side. —I'm going to live in New York. In two years' time, one way or another, that's what I'm *going to do.*

—Lucky Keith. I'd do it myself, if I had the chance.

They enroll in the same seminar, on "The American Renaissance." After a brief hesitation, Susan concedes to *Moby Dick*—the way, she says, you just have to concede to Blake; and when Keith reaches the bedroom scene with Queequeg, he gives in also. But then, Hawthorne? It becomes a game with them to recite to each other the egregiously ponderous bits:

—*It is a heavy annoyance to a writer, who endeavors to represent nature, its various attitudes and circumstances, in a reasonably correct outline and true coloring, that so much of the mean and ludicrous should be hopelessly mixed up with the purest pathos...*

—Oh, bloody hell, mate, get the fuck on with it! Right, here's one for you, Suze: *This fair girl deemed herself conscious of a power—combined of beauty, high, unsullied purity, and the preserv-*

ative force of womanhood—that could make her sphere impenetrable, unless betrayed by treachery within.

—*Preservative force?* Susan figures. —He must mean pickled in laudanum, the ladies' favorite treat of the times. Nice reference to penetration, though. Couldn't get away with that after Freud.

But Hawthorne will never fly for them—the stuff simply reeks of self-consciousness, a perpetual irritation—and at the same time he's so obviously *not on to himself.* That's the killer. Something of the same problem with Emerson, too, even Thoreau. There's a smell about this old New England sensibility that evokes too clearly those uninviting chapels in Midlands towns that they used to avoid by rocketing past on the train.

Weekends, penniless Susan stays on campus, writing letters and watching the beautiful undergraduates from a lonely distance. Keith, who has money sent from home, goes into Cambridge and Boston, and comes back now and then with adventures to report. Example: when Anthony Perkins is filming something in the area, and takes Keith up to his hotel room to give him a blow job (no mystery now to Susan).

—Have fun, then?

—Well, yes, flirting in the bar was lots of fun, says Keith. —And when we went to his room, I thought I did my bit okay. But he seemed in a hurry to get rid of me afterwards. Rather annoying.

Susan quotes Lili on celebrities, to console. —See, once they get on film, they're just not real people anymore.

There's a graduate student party at the end of the semester, where Susan gets drunk and goes to bed with a plausible guy from the American Lit. seminar who, after one straightforward routine, wakes her up in the wee hours pressing her to take it in the rear. That's what he really, really wants. But Susan puts him off, resorting to a new phrase she's learned, *Not on the first date.* And she doesn't like him enough for a second date, although she's grateful for the new information: this, too, is America, liking it best in the arse or the mouth—anywhere but the obvious.

She talks about it with Keith. His predictable view is that American men are mostly queer, but can't *fundamentally* admit it. Susan speculates otherwise: there's too many Catholics about the place, for one thing, and for another, the frightening level of endemic boredom, which she connects with the absence of pub life, of little cafés and shops, which connects in turn to the over-sized roads, and these vast distances between places.

Jim comes to Boston for three days of Christmas vacation, before going on to a conference in San Francisco. They make love in their familiar, satisfying way, which is oddly disconcerting to Susan, for in a strange land, even familiar things appear subtly changed. Three weeks later she writes to him that she's missed her period.

He writes back (is he psychic all of a sudden, or extrapolating from his own private adventures in Texas?) to say well, if she is pregnant, can she be absolutely sure that he's the father? He doesn't like to imply anything, but after those months apart, and given his scrupulosity about using a condom (even though she used a diaphragm), if there was, by chance, some *"altr'uomo"*—well, he'd have certain feelings about that—

The day after Jim's letter reaches her, making her blush with a half-guilty rage, Susan wakes up to find a bloodstain on her nightdress. The threat of pregnancy is over. She begins composing, first in her head, then on paper, her Dear Jim letter. In it, she takes all the blame, grovels in self-abasement for not staying the course, and regrets all the emotional carnage she has caused. But she's clear: it's over, it's absolutely gone. Jim's reply, in turn, lets her off charitably—even though she won't learn for another year that he has already met, down in Texas, the woman he'll soon call his Dark Lady, the great love of his life. Those two will never marry, either: that's how it is with Dark Ladies.

Jim and Susan continue to exchange Christmas cards every year, with a brief letter inside, and in this way she learns that Jim marries twice more, though he begets no children. Each wife in turn will happen to be named Susan. But Susan's aware that hers is one of the five commonest names for girls in America (Mary is number one), so one can hardly make much of it.

Keith seems to be the one most troubled by the breakup.

—I thought you guys had the real thing! he protests. —You went through all that *Sturm und Drang* to make this happen. And then, the moment marriage becomes a real possibility, you just blow it away. I am *so* disappointed in you, Susan.

—Perhaps I'm allergic to marriage. I'm sorry, Susan tells him, although she's dead-tired of apologies.

—Not only that, says Keith, —you've deprived me of one of my favorite lines in English verse, remember? *If Susan comes, can Jim be far behind?*

—Shut up, Keith. Don't depress me. Just because there aren't any classic poems with 'Keith' in them—and just because there's no Keith Shakespeare, Keith Wordsworth, Keith Keats!—

—Not yet, not yet—give me a little time!

—Anyway, says Susan, —you'll at least be glad to know I've decided on my romantic future. It's all settled. I'm going to marry America, warts and all. I shall bake hermits, and brownies, and have Tupperware parties, and be a den mother, all for lovely America. My sweetheart.

—That was fast work, says Keith. —As for me, I'll be happy just getting screwed by lovely America—

At the end of the year, Keith is worried. He has to visit his family in the U.K., and frankly, he looks so much more handsome, and more gay, than when he came over that it's a problem. He's developed a little muscle, playing tennis, and picked up a great tan. (Actually, Susan knows he uses a touch of facial bronzer, to enhance the effect.) When he goes out at night, he wears emerald-green contact lenses—a brilliant look. With his white tees, and his old cricket pullover, well, he's quite something. But how is he to face the parents?

On her side, Susan has scraped up barely enough money from her TA work, and serving as an experimental subject in psychology, to keep her dorm room for the summer. She's got a part-time job transcribing dictated field notes and paper revisions for a professor in sociology, which pays her food money. So Keith persuades her to take three weeks out of that for a trip home—he'll pick up her airfare, if she'll come to Yorkshire with him and play the role of "the girl I'm seriously interested in."

—This is very weird, Keith, but if it's that important to you—

—Well, I'm afraid it is.

—Then okay. I know how to do these things. I was actually engaged, once. I mean, before Jim.

There will be the shake-hands greeting at the station, the cold meat-loaf sandwiches from an old family recipe at lunch, the healthy walk and admiration of the scenery before tea, and the decidedly separate rooms at bedtime. Questions will be fielded adroitly—it'll be understood that Susan's family in suburban London is looking forward to meeting Keith also, the next week (when in fact, he'll be having a hellfire time around the old haunts). At the station again, a powdery goodbye kiss on the cheek, warm smiles, and the charade is over.

—Did it work okay? Susan asks him when they meet at the pub in St. Martin's Lane. He's utterly transformed again, of course, with the leather jacket and ultra jeans he'd left at a friend's.

—Thanks to you, I get a pass this time. Better give me your family stats, before I forget, so I can spin them the rest of it.

—Right. Got a notepad? Dad passed on a few years ago. Mum works in medical records, at local hospital. Two sisters, one older, one younger. Nurse, and generally fucked-up rock fan, respectively.

—Ah, come on!

—Okay, she's officially a vet's assistant. Likes animals. But you know something else? Our grocer at home took me for a Canadian—already. It's happening!

—But not to me, says Keith. —With you, I could tell the rot was setting in when you got that blouse with a round collar.

—What can I do? Just a porous person—

In three years, Keith and Susan have passed their comprehensive exams: they've learned to write respectful analyses of Hawthorne, and to compete in the job market. Keith has won his dream job, right there in Manhattan, at Fordham. Never mind, he says, if there are crucifixes on the wall—forget those—he can already feel the rumble of New York streets under his footsoles, the wind through the high-rise canyons, the crowds and more crowds. Susan's thesis director has helped her to a place upstate, at Mount Holyoke.

—I knew it wouldn't happen, she says. —When I was in England, I never managed to live in London proper. Now I'm here, I'll never manage to live in New York. Stupid, stupid. And I miss seeing Lili so much!

The next time Susan gets a long weekend in the city, she's with her new guy, and Lili explains over the phone that she's hooked up now with a radical lesbian, which means she can't be in a social encounter of any kind with a man. The two of them meet alone one afternoon, for coffee. But it's a sorry meeting, apart from interesting gossip about Judy Collins's private life. Lili has gained weight, and she doesn't even look as happy as her conversion had predicted. No matter how sympathetic Susan is, she's instructed that she has cast in her lot with the oppressor. In effect, she's damned herself—but wait, does she intend to marry this man? Well, that could happen, eventually. It could? Then there's no more to say on the subject, it's hopeless.

Two years further on, Susan sends Lili a birth announcement, out of courtesy, because Lili has sent her a change-of-address announcement (she's moved to a better place, on the western fringe of the Village proper). Susan also has moved, still in New England.

Another summer, and Lili calls to say she's coming north on assignment, to interview an actress on location, and can she stay on for a couple of nights, after she's filed the story? Men, she adds, don't bother her anymore; although she's still living with a woman, it's a different woman. Lili arrives with a clear plastic tote bag containing a toothbrush, hairbrush, a wig, and the extra black T-shirt (but to be sure, her professional makeup kit is carried in the maximum-sized purse). This time the connection is back: Lili greets her with a complete embrace, and needs no excuse of politeness to admire Susan's girl-child, at eighteen months a feminist's dream of joyously untrammeled self-will.

The second night, an operatic thunderstorm rolls overhead at four a.m. Susan wakes, and comes to sit in her living room (how strange, she thinks, with Lili under her roof, to find oneself a person with a living room—). There, Lili joins her—Lili, who was never woken by Manhattan's traffic, but who is genuinely scared by lightning and thunder. Susan gets them drinks, and they sit in the flickering dark while the storm passes on.

—I'll be moving again, next month, Lili says suddenly. —I love women, y'know, but living together doesn't work. And to be honest, what I really do like is to be penetrated. That's what I want.

Susan thinks for a moment. —Yeah, now that you remind me, I have to agree—there's nothing like it.

—I mean, there's dildos, and Julie uses a strap-on, so it's not a total loss that way, but it's still *plastic*—it isn't the same thing.

—It has to be penetration in the flesh—that other body, doesn't it?

—That's the thing I want. In the end. Which reminds me—

And Lili goes into a long riff on the personal history of a famous rock groupie she's close to. —So I finally tell her, You are *such a whore*! And she says to me, How can you *say* that, when I haven't had *anyone* since the Tremolos six months ago?

Rock music and musicians have become her great passion, the subject of the book which will make her name in New York and beyond, and give her almost everything she's ever wished for, but will also (as she tells it) take away her health. When Susan drives Lili to the station next day, she'll be seeing her once more only, in the exotic cave of a studio she's made for herself in the city—the place where she will die, recognized but alone, of an acute asthma attack.

Keith, who's living way uptown from Lili, in the Bronx, will not share even that degree of good fortune. True, he writes Susan one letter from Fordham, where he's a popular teacher of what they call there British Lit., indicating that New York's pleasures and adventures exceed his wildest dreams. "Wildest" is underlined.

But even as Susan herself is losing track of time, immersed in the heroics of mothering, the baking of hermits and brownies, arranging of Tupperware parties, the news comes to her by way of Joel, whom she's forgotten from graduate school, but who got her number through the alumni network. It's about Keith, he's been found dead. Took an immense overdose of sleeping pills, and died two days ago. It's even worse than that, Joel tells her, because if he were not dead, he'd be facing charges of attempted murder of his roommate, whom he attacked earlier that night with a tire iron, and left with a smashed face and skull fractures, and who's still in a coma.

Keith. The boyish man who wrote those poems verging on over-sweetness—one of them (where is it now?) dedicated to Susan herself. Her ironic friend, Keith, who had only enough muscles to look good on the tennis court. And now she remembers Joel was the guy who obtained a couple of tabs of acid one year, but it was Keith who insisted on cutting Susan in on the party, so they each got two-thirds of a tab. They took the acid together, with beer chasers. Forty minutes later, she decided against the experience.

—This stuff is some kind of poison, she recalls saying, and recalls the sensation, too: the brain caught in some kind of brutal vise, and the escalating conviction of utter helplessness.

Joel just sat there, morosely absorbed as usual, but Keith was positively ebullient.

—Wow! he kept saying. —Wow, wow! This stuff is extremely different, I would say—it's got some definite zing to it! I can positively recommend this!

Then she got up to leave.

—Hey, Suze! Keith said. —You aren't supposed to leave, baby, it's against the rules, we're supposed to stay together, you know—

But she left anyway, walking half-blinded by the weird green glow over everything, got back to her room, and lay down for a night of dreadful imprisonment, immobilized on her back, staring at the pulsating bars of light the venetian blinds cast upward on the ceiling.

Then the city gave Keith all the drugs he could ever want, and all the sex he'd ever craved. *I'll be happy just getting screwed by lovely America.*

Decades later, Susan meets again the Jewish joke that she first heard in New York, the one that ended with the line *Pity we lost India.* It is offered up at a dinner party by the French *maître à penser,* Professor D. There are minor variations in detail along the way, but the outcome is identical—the old fellow drawing himself up in his new Bond Street suit, trying out the air of a sahib—and produces once more a burst of general laughter, in which Susan joins.

By now, she's had much time to consider the random oddity of how things went: leaving an England stripped down to all but its territorial underwear, only to witness imperial America's dissolving into corporate globalism. Susan imagines turning to Lili now, or Keith or Jim, but there's no one to count on understanding how it felt, floating absently across the world while empires foundered under them.... On the other hand, she has this reassurance that, like her fellow professional aliens, she finally does get the punchline.

Mothy Ode

One of those pizza-like images of the moons of Jupiter
before computer enhancement is how I look to this moth,
since that's how everything looks (see Monet, etcetera)
before the brain, with help from personal history,
cleans it up. And this moth, the poor trustee
of one small fraction of a thought, has got no room
in its two-byte brain for *This* or *Feed?* or *Breed!*
and *Clean it up* together. And as to history: *Huh?*

So I'm *Bulk, vertical,* joined firmly to the earth,
the same as a bookcase or a tree. This pleases me.
Does a moth see depth? I guess it would have to
to steer boldly among stems to find whatever it finds
(what do moths eat, anyway, nectar? air? ignorance?)

Its life must be a video driving game,
cartoon-like obstacles rising up, its own swerving
difficult to tell from the roads. It can't have room
for the thought *I'm steering* as it steers, giddily,
down the slope of pheromone concentrations
in something that feels like providential falling.
Something thinks *for* it, the moth would think, if it could think.

From a moth's angle, I am the sheer heft
of Othernness, in all its inexplicable wonder.
Everything about me is pure instress, startling me-ness,
my gaffes and hesitation wired from birth.
Even the frantic waving of my arms, Hey *Moth!*
seems to declare me a creature of pure nature,
though it looks to me like considerable calculation.

In tragic opposition, some Super-Moth might mourn,
the quality of Mothness is fixate on high contrast
and, surging again and again (in a kind of software crash)
into romantic candles, or unromantic porchlights,
roast and pulverize. Ah, this is beauty, all the soul can take
of passion's endless loop! Which is not so pleasing.

Whereas a human's amazingly fluid slowness (to a moth)
reveals a being unburdened by desire (like a stone
I would say, but moths don't notice stones) and wedded,
by a massiveness beyond conception, to the planet,
or, as their apostrophe to us goes,

Anchor,
wind-strayed never,
into no sun falling,
daystander, pure endurer
of the dazzling brilliance of our drives...

or something like that, and we who can sit so long,
looking at pages (as far as *they* can tell) of darkness,
we with the calm of oceans and things too slow to be visible,
we who are indistinguishable from each other,
how could we suffer reverses? Well may they whirr at my screens

Thou was not born for death, immortal human—
the bulk I see this passing night was seen
by ancient Polyphemus, hawk moth, luna...

in ultrasonic worship. Why *shouldn't* I,
since they ask so little, mime, as for my children,
a simplicity that might ease their faith?
The god-part comes naturally: *O little ones!*
hear my thunderous speech, each word long as a moth-life.
The flame I look upon unmoved. Also the porchlight.
All that your flitteriness leaves ungrasped,
I hold upon, practically an Assistant Planet.
I am the blindness with which the Universe

beholds itself and knows itself divine.
I am the huge unmoving root
of that body of which you, O jittery ones,
are the tips of the fingertips, and when I ponder
I grow perfect as darkness, disappearing. There.

Movie Review

Fatherhood is like dying.
A flood of days pools at the neck.
Glub.
He was born on the *th* of June.
In the movie version, ghostly Jennifer Jason Leigh
sits at the bus station,
strung out, penniless, blowing cigarette smoke
at the bruises on her distant, fetal legs,
and dreaming of an Academy Award.
Careful watching discovers it's an airport
and she's not allowed on the plane
because she doesn't have shoes.
A man in a suit, probably a ticket agent, restrains her.
She begs, sobs, screams, prays at the top of her lungs.
Doesn't anybody want to give me a pair of shoes!
Fucking shoes. Please!
until my baby son,
or a boy in the airport, gives her his black sneakers.
He is premature, eight weeks old, and will love the forlorn
and the desperate. What can I do to save him?
Now he invokes his lizard tongue
in the center of his own preverbal sobbing.
In the living-room version, I am Jennifer Jason Leigh,
a weather update
and Hurricane Jennifer fibrillates. It's a role with broad range,
and her instrument is her body. It's a ripe raspberry
vibrating at the center of a cave.
His amnion was a cave full of dark sounds.
His mother's uterus. The sonar pinging of love
or guitar strings. Jennifer Jason Leigh sings off-key.
Understand this, and you may begin to understand the movie.
What we want we cannot have. In Maslow's hierarchy of needs
my tongue is a strawberry.

He was less than a minute old when I held his hand.
The colors of sunset washed through him a blue at a time.
He smelled of butter and crackled like bacon. His breath
salted the air, and the days began to pool.
Call it a flood again. Water is the most abundant metaphor on Earth,
but money is more basic than food or shelter.
The waves and gurges of his cries
coin around me.

Ophthalmology at Dawn

for Gregory J. Pamel, M.D.

Dawn is ugly, a fug over day,
a tarpaulin
on a top-of-the-line motorcycle.

An amaryllis
has a hideous nativity:
two shoots peer from the bulb

frantically as a chick
peers out of its ovular jail.
Beginnings are rarely pretty:

think of sperm, woolly
mammoths, pre-atmospheric
goo. Beginning, too,

is the hardest part of work,
so dawn is another affront
like taxes, insurance, or rent.

Still, the amaryllis that erupts
so horrifically from its bulb
does eventually unfold

a dazzling, two-headed
megaphone.
And in the machinery

of ophthalmology
the retina is a forest at dusk,
reddening beneath the beaming

optic disc. The eye
is diachronic because it sees
the past in everything

and because it's a planet
with a setting sun
no matter the time of day.

Diva Atonement Tour #1

I hate the psyche.
Cloudy today: brown, carmine, and blue.

I'm having a devilish time
controlling my body's

two gods:
theatric, tutelary.

Last night I decided again
to be a maniac, risking brain

fever, like my father,
whose temperature once rose to 108:

impressive. In our house,
only the sick were great.

German Romantic Song

Cryptic owl on my sill,
olive branch in the gold-bowered cope,

when I was a child I didn't know
what the word "colleague" meant: darkness?
My father had many colleagues;
I had none.

I told his assistant, twenty-one years ago,
"I wonder which I love most,
words or music."
I can't remember her advice,
though later she sued my father—
a long story. Perhaps
ecstasy can't be sought?
Materialism is no longer my amour,
I'm forever a bridegroom to bliss and its disguises.

Sestina: Bob

According to her housemate, she is out with Bob
tonight, and when she's out with Bob
you never know *when* she'll get in. Bob
is an English professor. Bob
used to be in a motorcycle gang, or something, or maybe Bob
rides a motorcycle now. How radical of you, Bob—

I wish I could ride a motorcycle, Bob,
and also talk about Chaucer intelligently. Bob
is very tall, bearded, reserved. I saw Bob
at a poetry reading last week—he had such a Bob-
like poise—so quintessentially Bob!
The leather jacket, the granny glasses, the beard—Bob!

and you were with my ex-girlfriend, Bob!
And you're a professor, and I'm nobody, Bob,
nobody, just a flower-deliverer, Bob,
and a skinny one at that, Bob—
and you are a large person, and I am small, Bob,
and I hate my legs, Bob,

but why am I talking to you as if you were here, Bob?
I'll try to be more objective. Bob
is probably a nice guy. Or that's what one hears. Bob
is not, however, the most passionate person named Bob
you'll ever meet. Quiet, polite, succinct, Bob
opens doors for people, is reticent in grocery stores. Bob

does not talk about himself excessively to girlfriends. Bob
does not have a drinking problem. Bob
does not worry about his body, even though he's a little heavy.
   Bob
has never been in therapy. Bob,

also, though, does not have tenure—ha ha ha—*and* Bob
cannot cook as well as I can. Bob

never even heard of paella, and if he had, Bob
would not have changed his facial expression at all. Bob
is just so boring, and what I can't understand, Bob—
yes I'm talking to you again, is why you, Bob,
could be more desirable than me. Granted, Bob,
you're more stable, you're older, more mature *maybe* but Bob . . .

(Months later, on the Bob-front: My former girlfriend finally
   married Bob.
Of Bob, she says, "No one has taken me higher or lower than
   Bob."
Me? On a dark and stormy sea of Bob-thoughts, desperately,
   I bob.)

Social Life

After the party ends another party begins
and the survivors of the first party climb
into the second one as if it were a lifeboat
to carry them away from their slowly sinking ship.

Behind me now my friend Richard
is getting a fresh drink, putting on more music,
moving from group to group—smiles and
jokes, laughter, kissy-kiss—

It is not given to me to understand
the social pleasures of my species, but I think
what he gets from these affairs
is what bees get from flowers—a nudging of the stamen,

a sprinkle of pollen
about the head and shoulders—

whereas I prefer the feeling of going away, going away,
stretching out my distance from the voices and the lights
until the tether breaks and I

am in the wild sweet dark
where the sea breeze sizzles in the hedgetop
and the big weed heads whose names I never learned
lift and nod upon their stalks.

What I like about the trees is how
they do not talk about the failure of their parents
and what I like about the grasses is that
they are not grasses in recovery

and what I like about the flowers is
that they are not flowers in need of
empowerment or validation. They sway

upon their thorny stems
as if whatever was about to happen next tonight
was sure to be completely interesting—

the moon rising like an ivory tusk,
a few funky molecules of skunk
strolling through the air
to mingle with the aura of a honeysuckle bush,

and when they bump together in my nose,
I want to raise my head and sing,
I'm a child in paradise again
when you touch me like that, baby,

but instead, I stand still and listen
to the breeze departing from the upper story of a tree
and the hum of insects in the field,
letting everything else have a word, and then another word,

because silence is always good manners
and often a clever thing to say
when you are at a party.

Rumors: Poetry

The air turns red: rumors of sex, death rumors,
rumors of rumors, offering their feigned collective
sympathy. *So sad she dumped her latest husband...*
Tragic that he showed up sloshed (again!)—
at the wedding reception, staggered into the cake,
face-down at the tiny feet of the sugar couple...

Poets' lives: *Who fucked the judge and won the prize?* Coupled
on the Internet: hot progress, cruel dualities, undenied. Rumor:
X gets paid big six-figure bread. But it's obvious, stale cake's
what the rest get! These days, you need a critic or a collective
politics to reinvent yourself. Not just once—again and again,
like sexual exploits repositioned on the john door. Husband

your vines, tend to your metaphors. Listen to the husband
of the Muse: Virgil, poet-god & Caesar's ass-kisser. Coupling
epic clash with epic trash? Once we were high-minded. Again,
a reformed satyr writes his memoirs, proving the self's a rumor.
Or witness the sadist, incest-victim, twelve-step-collective
careerist icing his sweet, pain-studded lyrics, like poison cakes.

Once I jumped naked from a cake.
Once I fucked someone, not my husband.
Once I joined a hippie collective.
Once I broke up a supposedly happy couple.
Once I slashed my wrists (one of these rumors
is not true). Once I rose to Hell then sank again

in the elevator of a penthouse prison. Again,
why's each newcomer a bright backstabbing climber? Cake:
piece of. There's a log-rolling in the *Times*. Rumor
as politics. *X sexually harassed all genders in his class, husband*

only to his pet ferret. Some suck up to academics. Who couples
with whom shouldn't matter. It's the work! This great collective

love of what we do! Sentimental first-person plural collective:
We. Us. Together we stand...(And piss in the Aeolian wind again
and again.) *So everyone thought it was her best poem*...(Uncoupled
from her sagging, varicose line breaks, that is. Or uncaked
from her experimentalist droppings, sex-changed, husbanded
by a new Zeus of Ideology.) *Would he/she/I lie to you?* Rumor:

*The widespread X-stasy rumor proved untrue. Ditto a collective
fantasy about HER husband, HIS partner, SOMEONE'S kid. Again:
Must a couple hundred eggs break, before we serve literary cake?*

Lupine, Clear Place

desire   prize   ambition   lakeside

      lupine,

               clear place—

———

For a minute prizes didn't matter because the black and white
    spider sat in the daisy.

Two ducks along the shore that the ice storm had ravaged,
    so that there were more blue lupine than before—

And in fact everything was more vivid because it had once
    suffered defeat: the rocks were blooming,
        there were less places to sit—

For a long time the prize was a clear place to sit, inside of all
    that was resurging—

So that winning equaled the dust-blue tails of lupine?

When you had been thinking it was more like the man
    kayaking out there,
        against the triangular wakes of the speedboats—

For a minute the prize was forgetting about it. For a minute
    the lake's silver page—

field that was mirroring creation—

that there was a clear place to sit,
        inside of all that wanting—

Days of 1986

He was believed by his peers to be an important poet,
But his erotic obsession, condemned and strictly forbidden,
Compromised his standing, and led to his ruin.

Over sixty, and a father many times over,
The objects of his attention grew younger and younger:
He tried to corrupt the sons of his dearest friends;
He pressed on them drinks and drugs,
And of course he was caught and publicly shamed.
Was his death a suicide? No one is sure.

But that's not the whole story; it's too sordid to tell.
Besides, the memory of his poems deserves better.
Though we were unable to look at them for a time
His poems survive his death.
There he appears as his finest self:
Attractive, scholarly, dedicated to love.

At last we can read him again, putting aside
The brute facts of his outer life,
And rejoice at the inner voice, so lofty and pure.

The Impossible May Be Possible

Stone calcifies around it
creating an impenetrable shell.
In spite of its heaviness it floats
somewhere in her body
though she is never quite sure where
until she stops to think about it.
Probing, probing, hoping this time,
this time that when she feels it bang
against a rib or whack her heart,
this time she can crack it open,
find the happiness that should be
floating through her unprotected
by a shell, like someone looking
through a telescope and—is that?—
could it be?—a new star? Bright:
this has been a week of wonders;
she knows it has. But that is all.
To know and not to feel turns joy
to sadness like apple juice to vinegar.
She reaches for a glass of vinegar
and drinks it down, hoping it will coat
the stony shell and weaken it enough
so it will crack and fall away in pieces.
Imprisoned feeling will flood out:
a river curling like a marcel wave
and in its blues sunlight reflecting—
as she does, perhaps too sharp
or dim—an old star genuflecting.

Pussy Willow (An Apology)

Why delay? Today I stopped
to rub the fur, like the tender
ear of a cat, stopped

to stroke the lush gray
plush (and oh, the pink!) as if
the cat had rasped

itself to frenzy, to an
ecstasy of itch
all raw

this steak tartar, this
chafe of meat, and
because of this

I was late (the willows in
their bins outside
the florist almost as tall as I)

and once again, have traded
friendship for
dillydally.

I had to take off
my gloves, and I would have
taken off my skin

(for why should I put
a barrier between
myself and anything?)

to pluck, to blow back
each separate tuft
of foam (in down, sink down)

because I cannot keep my hands
off the world and the world
out of my breath. What

does the world want (anyway)
of me with its pussy willows, with
its tears and angers

its greeds and splendors, its
petitions of
skyscrapers and waterfalls?

And what do I want with
its famous and forgotten? And is
this the purpose of my life,

to figure this out? Or is it
to touch and be touched? And if
I love the world more than

any one person, or if I love
one person more
than the world, what

does this say of me?
And what do I say to friends
when they keep me waiting,

Oh dally, friend, delight
so that I may rub
it from your body

its furs and gewgaws, its
horrors and sweetnesses, so you may
deliver it to me, you

the messenger, the unwinged
the prosaic in all
its scratch and bliss?

ABOUT MARK DOTY

A Profile by Mark Wunderlich

A summer visitor to the Cape Cod resort village of Province-town, Massachusetts, is liable to see just about anything walking down Commercial Street, the town's main drag and zone of street theater. From muscle boys with shaved chests and nail polish to Portuguese fishermen in waders to a drag queen wearing a G-string, metal helmet, and gold body paint, the possibilities for human identities seem both fluid and vast. P-town is also a site of incredible natural beauty, but a volatile one. Surrounded on three sides by water, the tip of the Cape is pounded by waves and winter storms, its shape shifting as the wind moves the dunes. In the summer, it is a circus, in the winter, desolate. It is this landscape of both natural and human extremity and theatricality that the poet Mark Doty uses as the surface upon which to map an inner life.

The author of five collections of poems and a memoir, Mark Doty is one of the most celebrated writers of his generation—the winner of a National Book Critics Circle Award and the first American to earn the T. S. Eliot Prize in Britain. He has also received a Whiting Writer's Award, fellowships from the Guggenheim Foundation and the NEA, and the Witter Bynner Poetry Prize from the American Academy of Arts & Letters.

Born in Maryville, Tennessee, in 1953, Doty spent much of his childhood moving around the country. His father was a civilian member of the Army Corps of Engineers, and the job required one relocation after another. The place where Doty first came in contact with contemporary poetry was Tucson, Arizona, where he went to high school. A drama teacher introduced him to the poet Richard Shelton, who read Doty's early poems and encouraged him. "Most importantly," Doty says, "he showed me that one could have a life as a poet, that literature, or any art, might be the very center of one's experience." No small trick in Tucson, in the suburbs in the sixties. One moment in particular stayed in Doty's memory. "I went to Dick Shelton's house in the desert to help clean out his garage, and his wife, Lois, was at the piano when I walked in, playing Kurt Weill and singing 'Pirate Jenny' from *The Threepenny Opera* in German. I felt a window had opened onto another world."

During the seventies, while living in Iowa, where he'd attended Drake University, he cowrote and published three chapbooks with his then-wife, the poet Ruth Doty—books to which he no longer feels an allegiance. He now thinks of *Turtle, Swan* as his first book. Published in 1987 by David R. Godine, *Turtle, Swan* announced the arrival of a singular and vibrantly new voice in American poetry. These early poems were marked with what have come to be signatures of Doty's work: an efficient narration of events, an elegant handling of free verse one wants to call "post-formal," and a lyric intensity akin to that of Doty's prominent influence, Hart Crane. The book was not simply a precursor of things to come, but evidence of a voice fully formed. One of the most notable poems in the collection is the extraordinary "Charlie Howard's Descent," which describes the 1984 killing of a homosexual man who was thrown from a bridge by a group of boys in Bangor, Maine:

> Over and over
> he slipped into the gulf
> between what he knew and how
> he was known

With these lines, Doty took bold steps toward becoming the first post-Stonewall gay poet to emerge as a major voice in American letters. His predecessors, such as James Merrill, William Meredith, and Richard Howard, had all favored a more privileged tone and vocabulary, elaborate ventriloquism through personae, or occluded references to homosexuality. On the opposite spectrum, Ginsberg used an expansive self-mythologizing strung along an elastic line to address topics that placed him on America's sexual margins. With *Turtle, Swan*, Doty effectively merged the political with the aesthetic, uniting a taut line with a lyric voice and an imagination that included notions of activism. Simply by being open about his sexuality, by using it as a subject for his poems without having it be *the* subject, Doty created a new model for gay and lesbian poets and poetry.

Ted Rosenberg

For several years, Doty and his partner, Wally Roberts, lived in Montpelier, Vermont. Doty taught creative writing at Goddard College, where he'd received his M.F.A., and he and Wally renovated a one-hundred-ten-year-old house. In 1989, Wally tested positive for HIV. Doty tested negative. In his bestselling memoir about Wally's illness and decline, *Heaven's Coast* (HarperCollins, 1996), Doty writes, "The virus seemed to me, first, like a kind of solvent which dissolved the future, our future, a little at a time. It was like a dark stain, a floating, inky transparency hovering over Wally's body, and its intention was to erase the time ahead of us, to make that time, each day, a little smaller." In 1989 the couple visited Provincetown, renting a house on the beach, and eventually decided to stay. The beautiful seaside environment, and the sizable gay community that could provide support for the couple as they faced Wally's illness together, made it seem an ideal place to settle.

In his second volume of poems, *Bethlehem in Broad Daylight* (David R. Godine, 1991), Doty began chronicling Provincetown, its light and harbor and glittering surfaces. More than rare beauty distinguished the poems, however. One got the sense that Doty now viewed poetry as an arena of argument—an argument between public and private selves about how to construct an inner life. Most remarkable in this second book is the way in which observation of the physical world is integrated into a deeply personal and intimate narrative.

In 1993, Mark Doty's third volume of poems was selected by Philip Levine for the National Poetry Series and published by the University of Illinois Press. *My Alexandria* (the title of which makes reference to another primary Doty influence, C. P. Cavafy) was a tour de force, catapulting Doty into the center of attention. The book is perhaps the finest in-depth literary investigation of the AIDS crisis, and at its center is the anticipation of tremendous loss, an ache that pervades each of the poems. Curiosity about the incidental leads to inner investigations of the relationship between sex and illness, desire and inevitable decay. In the long poem "The Wings," Doty begins with a description of a boy at an auction, lying on the grass, reading. As the poem progresses, he offers:

> Don't let anybody tell you
>
> death's the price exacted
> for the ability to love;
>
> couldn't we live forever
> without running out of occasions?

Both readers and critics responded generously to *My Alexandria.* The book received numerous awards, including *The Los Angeles Times* Book Award and the National Book Critics Circle Award. Yet Doty's success was to be shadowed by loss. In February of 1994, his partner, Wally, died of complications from AIDS. Doty writes, "In some way I had joined the invisible, too. I think that when people die they make those around them feel something like they felt; that may be the dying's first legacy to us.... Acceptance breeds acceptance, as Wally's attitude during his illness had shown; it'd been easy, somehow, for the people who took care of him to do so. He seemed, to those who carried him, to have made himself light."

In *Atlantis,* published in 1995 by HarperCollins, Doty documents with great acuity the colors and textures of Provincetown.

The book describes storm after storm. Ruined boats are both ravishing and haunted. Each tempest leaves behind something beautiful, but tinged with sorrow. It is a book about a storm, and the storm's quiet aftermath; something has been lost, but something else is left behind, worthy of description and contemplation. Punctuating the volume are occasional spikes of rage, as in the poem "Homo Will Not Inherit," in which the poet confronts a flier stating, "Homo will not inherit. Repent and be saved."

> ...I have for hours
> believed—without judgment, without condemnation—
> that in each body, however obscured or recast,
>
> is the divine body—common, habitable—
> the way in a field of sunflowers
> you can see every bloom's
>
> the multiple expression
> of a single shining idea,
> which is the face hammered into joy.

This is Doty at the height of his powers, the poem driven into the world by force of the poet's will, the engine hurtling it along his ecstatic imagistic capabilities. He turns biblical language on its ear, reclaiming its strength and lyricism, while exposing its misuse as an instrument of hate. The book's primary subject remains grief and its survival—loss as it scours the psyche to the bone.

With *Sweet Machine* (HarperCollins, 1998), Doty's most recent book, we see a poet emerging with a more public voice, a formidable and lyrical style of argumentation. "I'm wanting my own poems to turn more towards the social, to the common conditions of American life in our particular uncertain moment," Doty says. "I am, I guess, groping towards those poems; I'm trying to talk about public life without resorting to public language."

"Mercy on Broadway" from *Sweet Machine* acts as a bridge, linking Doty's previous work with his new artistic ambitions. The poet takes on the tumult and rapture of Manhattan, describing a scene on lower Broadway, where a woman is trying to sell a bowl full of turtles from a place on the sidewalk:

...I'm forty-one years old
and ready to get down

on my knees to a kitchen bowl
full of live green. I'm breathing here,

a new man next to me who's beginning
to matter.

The poem becomes a meditation on finding the will to start over, but it also functions as a love song for the noise and chaos of street life as it shuffles itself into and out of meaning. In this masterful poem, Doty combines the vast and the very small, what's impersonal and what is deeply felt.

Mark Doty makes his living as a teacher of creative writing, and in recent years he has taught at the Iowa Writers' Workshop, Columbia University School of the Arts, and the creative writing program at the University of Utah. He currently teaches one semester a year at the University of Houston, and he and his partner, the novelist Paul Lisicky, split their time between Houston and Provincetown.

Doty recently finished a second memoir entitled *Firebird*, which will be published by HarperCollins next year. "*Firebird* is an autobiography from six to sixteen, with a particular eye towards matters of aesthetic education: How do we learn to identify what we find beautiful, and what are the uses to which beauty is put? It's a sissy boy's story, and thus an exile's tale, and a chronicle of a gradual process of coming to belong somewhere, to the world of art." He goes on to add, "I hope the book is not so much about me as it is an examination of a whole constellation of experiences and ideas—personal and collective—about art, sexuality, identity, gender, and the survival of the inner life."

On summer afternoons in Provincetown, students from the Cape Cod School of Art are seen throughout the town, painting landscapes of various local scenes. Very often, groups of them set up easels in the street in front of Mark Doty and Paul Lisicky's two-century-old house. With its rose arbor, white clapboards, and vibrant, overblown flower beds, it's the perfect New England subject. With each stroke, the painters try to get at something Doty noted in his poem "Fog"—"some secret amplitude...in this orderly space"—which exemplifies what Doty has been able to reveal, with grace and mastery, in his work and life.

Mark Wunderlich is the author of the poetry collection The Anchorage, *which will be published this spring by the University of Massachusetts Press. He is currently a Wallace Stegner Fellow at Stanford University and the managing director of the Napa Valley Writers' Conference.*

Recommended Books · Spring 1999

PARADISE, NEW YORK *A novel by Eileen Pollack. Temple Univ. Press, $27.95 cloth. Reviewed by Fred Leebron.*

In her first novel, *Paradise, New York*, Eileen Pollack, author of the acclaimed 1991 story collection *The Rabbi in the Attic*, deftly evokes the entertaining and complex life of a Catskills hotel, as seen through the eyes of a young Jewish woman coming of age both spiritually and sexually.

Lucy Appelbaum is the third generation of the family who runs the Garden of Eden, a rambling and somewhat shabby hotel located near the town of Paradise, New York. To be sure, it is a quirky hotel, and when Lucy takes charge of it at age nineteen, it becomes quirkier still, filled with a cranky grandmother, out-of-date communists, and a cast of misfits and philosophers from which Pollack has wrought not only a comedy of errors, but also a serious tale about what it means to belong in the modern world.

Lucy's insights into the politics of sex are priceless and timeless. Eying a middle-aged insurance adjustor who has already seduced her once, she perceives that "like most unmarried men his age he seemed only half-tame, like a squirrel or a fox you're tempted to pet. And it came to me then that understanding why you had slept with such a man had nothing to do with whether you would give in and sleep with him again. . . . In Jimmy's mind, pleasure and business were as near to one another as his pockets to his genitals."

The real stake of the novel does not lie in whether Lucy can save the hotel from its fate of abandonment and destruction, but whether she can save herself from a descent into nihilism and inertia. For her own spiritual growth, she comes to rely on the sage black handyman, Thomas Jefferson, and during the course of the novel, the two dance a wonderfully subtle and at times bitter pas de deux that is both intellectually and sexually seductive. In their on-again, off-again, sometimes romantic friendship, Lucy finds a meaning not only in trying to save the Eden, but in her life as well. "A human being," Thomas eulogizes near the end of the novel, "doesn't come ready made. Person has to gather the pieces himself."

Lucy's struggle is to gather such pieces: what it means to be a woman, what it means to be Jewish, and what it means to try to transcend her sense of the limitations of both of these elements of her humanity. A Holocaust historian at the hotel to interview a few survivors chides one of them who will not talk, asking, "But who will tell your story after you're gone?"

"Story?" the survivor repeats. "What I have lived through is not a story."

While *Paradise, New York* is indeed the story of Lucy's coming of age in the detritus of the late 1970's Catskill resort industry, it is more than that, a tragicomic journey out of a world that cannot keep her and into a world that will not have her. Despite its lapses into glib comedy and explicit philosophizing, it is an ambitious and fully realized novel.

Fred Leebron is author of the novel Out West *and co-editor of* Postmodern American Fiction: A Norton Anthology. *His new novel,* Six Figures, *is forthcoming from Knopf in January 2000.*

BARDO *Poems by Suzanne Paola. Univ. of Wisconsin Press, $10.95 paper. Reviewed by Susan Conley.*

In Tibetan, the bardo is defined as a transitory state after death, a murky time where, Suzanne Paola writes in her latest book of poems, "the soul wanders through the heavens and hells...trying to achieve nirvana or Buddhahood." Selected for the 1998 Brittingham Prize in Poetry by Donald Hall, *Bardo* chronicles Paola's own complex journey from drug addiction to university tenure and motherhood. The speaker of these intriguing poems has chosen life over death, and there is a kind of awed, disbelieving celebration going on in *Bardo,* a book where "spirits hang all around" and traditional narrative forms undergo many face lifts.

The speaker of these disjointed, non-linear riffs has lived a life as "someone [she'd] be afraid of" and someone "she can't really remember." Paola's bardo is about a return from that drug-induced purgatory, where the trick is to "become basic, rendered / like a carcass in a farmwife's hands: into the pot / this huge thing, life, & out of it / a small substance: mostly fat & bone, / fat & bone" ("In the Realm of Neither Notions Nor Not Notions").

Many of these poems indeed paint stark pictures of heroin use, of boys with "a needle just into a vein," long after pop songs and poems about heroin have come to feel passé. However, what saves this collection, and what makes it such an important book, is its reinvention of the narrative confession—its unwillingness to render the somewhat familiar territory of drug addiction and dysfunction in any predictable fashion.

Paola subverts the conventional structure with odd crystallizations and wild thematic leaps. Life to this poet is an "elegant flow of one thing to the next," and Paola arranges *Bardo* with similar fluidity. Drugs or not, these poems trace how the mind works, how unpredictable its associations are, how creative its remaking of the past. This storytelling—a postmodern hybrid of lyric and narrative, with all kinds of religious deviations—makes for a haunting read. What could come off as heavy-handed and overtly self-conscious is largely effective because of Paola's spare language and evocative imagery. She details car crashes while high on mescaline, parties with "children staring at colors scarving from their hands...Frail-veined girls/who shot up in the webs of their fingers,/in the skull behind the ear," the idea being to "live anonymous to yourself."

Interspersing the vivid pastiche of drug use with teachings from Tibetan Buddhism, Paola parallels the spiritual journey with that of addiction: "How much heroin did it take to become selfless?/...How much Orange Crush & methadone?...Forgetting/how to strike a match, what my hands do." The Buddhist teachings rarely feel preachy, instead adding to the complexity and depth of the poet's search to reinterpret her life. In "Mistaking Opiates for the Clear Light," she writes: "I trust in the bardo wisdom: how the gods,/with their soft white light, draw us in, convince us/their stuporous world is all there is.//I've seen them, slumping/forward, burning themselves with cigarettes." Paola often wisely juxtaposes herself and her dark world of death and drugs with the bright, sober world of the living. Quaaludes, in their "eucharistic form" and "clear bags of heroin," are compared to a bowl of fruit: "A pear & a pomegranate wizen/into color. Almost/alive, skins racking." Paola "was their opposite, pale girl, not living or dying..."

In the aptly titled poem "Tenure at Forty," a welcome respite from the needle tracks and drug amnesia, the collection makes the thematic leap to a day job in academia, where the speaker "pulls on nude pantyhose to stand before the dean./Tenure meaning held."

Experimental California poet Carla Harryman wrote, "Narrative exists, and arguments either for or against it are false." Likewise, in *Bardo* Suzanne Paola seems to have come to terms with her own compulsion to weave tales. As innovative as the poems in this collection get, they do have a story to tell, and wisely they don't abandon that assignment.

In the end, this is a courageous book, portraying addiction and survival without being elegiac—without the self-importance that can contain and close off so much of American narrative poetry. This is a book that embraces limbo and the shock of having picked life over death, of having made it to the other side: "to have walked through the six realms/& somehow without knowing it/have chosen..."

THE FOREIGN STUDENT *A novel by Susan Choi. HarperFlamingo, $23.00 cloth. Reviewed by Don Lee.*

At first, finding any similarities between South Korea and Tennessee in the 1950's might seem impossible, but Susan Choi manages to do just that in her lyrical first novel, *The Foreign Student.*

In 1955, Chang Ahn flees war-battered Seoul and arrives at the University of the South in Sewanee, courtesy of a scholarship from the Episcopal Church Council. Shy and diffident, he is often baffled by the strangeness of Southern culture and people, from his roommate whose wealthy father is a Klansman, to the protocol involved when fraternizing with the colored help, to questions from curious church members, one of whom asks Chang, quite sincerely, if Koreans live in trees. Everywhere he goes, Chang feels "a subtle, unremitting scrutiny, disguised as politeness...varying in tone or intensity but always bringing with it the same slight electrification, as if he weren't just caught in a narrow beam of light but somehow animated by it." It becomes preferable to Chang to withdraw, burying himself in his calculus studies. He knows no one could comprehend his past, his nightmarish memories of the Korean War. His father, a professor who once enjoyed privilege and status, was imprisoned and disgraced; Chang's best friend, a communist, disappeared as a fugitive; and Chang himself, after working as a translator for the U.S. Information Services, was accused of being a spy and tortured mercilessly.

In Sewanee, his only outside contact becomes Katherine Monroe, a lively New Orleans heiress who has ensconced herself in her family's old summer home. She, too, has a past. At fourteen, she began an affair with Charles Addison, her father's best friend, who teaches Shakespeare at the university and is nearly thirty years her senior. Despite being disowned by her mother, Glee, over the affair, Katherine has continued as Addison's mistress, living on proper society's margins. She and Chang are drawn to each other from their first meeting, discovering an affinity that transcends race and country, that has more to do with wounds and estrangement: "Sometimes she was sure that the distance she felt between them wasn't difference, but a wariness they both turned toward the world."

In Susan Choi's hands, Chang and Katherine, as they slowly fall in love, find that they—and the Souths of Korea and Tennessee—are not that different after all, both subject to lingering issues of class, family, race, and civil war. *The Foreign Student* is hardly a perfect book. It is too elliptical in structure, and Chang's "delicate courtesy" too often makes for a passive, opaque character. But the novel is well worth reading for its poetic language, its ambitious story, and the complexity invested in every relation.

Robert Boswell recommends *A Gram of Mars*, a first collection by Becky Hagenston: "Becky Hagenston writes with grace, conviction, and wit. The complex stories in this collection circle about the central question in our lives—coming to terms with our past, coming to terms with the present. The stories have the stuff of real life and display the craft of a veteran writer; it's hard to believe that this is a first book by a young author. *A Gram of Mars* is a literary gem." (Sarabande)

George Garrett recommends *Dogfight and Other Stories*, a first collection by Michael Knight: "An outstanding collection of ten stories, various in form and content, which have already won this young and gifted writer several awards." (Plume)

Marilyn Hacker recommends *The Woman Behind You*, poems by Julie Fay: "Julie Fay's *The Woman Behind You* is at once a superb manifestation of the contemporary possibilities of lyric poetry and a sustained and gripping narrative of a late-twentieth-century woman's life, exemplary in its specificities, picaresque in the geographic and erotic vicissitudes of its quest. Like one of the pluckier folk-tale heroines, Fay's speaker travels long distances in search of her true home, her mother tongue. There are two powerful dialogues implicit here: between an adult daughter and her mother, between the American enduring a kind of exile in her own country and the expatriate conscious that she is most 'American' in the life she chose elsewhere: their counterpoint creates the book's

unique music, earthy and elegiac, generous in its discoveries." (Pittsburgh)

DeWitt Henry recommends *Rabbit Fever*, stories by Geoffrey Clark: "Geoffrey Clark's new collection, *Rabbit Fever*, is rich with terrible beauties. His mature prose is fresh with sensory texture, sonority, wit, hard-learned truths, and precisely dramatized voice. The progress through the collection as well as the upper Michigan setting is reminiscent of Hemingway's *Men Without Women*, charting the trajectory from comings of age as a boy with hunting, cars, and girls, to marriage and a teaching career, to midlife confrontations with death and grief. The most stunning story is in fact too urgent to be fiction, a heart-wrenching account of the deaths of both the writer's mother and his mentor, the novelist Richard Yates." (Avisson)

Jane Hirshfield recommends *The Snow Watcher*, poems by Chase Twichell: "Chase Twichell's new poems are both austere and luminous, both quiet and deeply startling. Her encounter with contemplative mind yields a poetry unlike any other—a new integration of Zen practice and American experience, American sentences. An utterly compelling and extraordinary book." (Ontario)

Philip Levine recommends *Picnic, Lightning*, poems by Billy Collins: "For some years now Billy Collins has been our most delightful poet, someone who handles his lines with superb grace and an unerring ear and whose personal take on the world can make the reader laugh out loud and beg for more. But careful readers of this new book will discover he is more than that; he is also a poet of great depth and profound mystery. Read such poems as 'Passengers,' 'Marginalia,' 'What I Learned Today,' and 'I Go Back to the House for a Book,' and you'll believe." (Pittsburgh)

Thomas Lux recommends *The Forgiveness Parade*, poems by Jeffrey McDaniel: "A terrifying, hilarious, and utterly alive second book by a young poet still in his early thirties. Read this book. If you get a chance to hear him read/perform, don't miss it: he can do it on the stage *and* on the page." (Manic D)

Maura Stanton recommends *Crossing*, a first novel by Manuel Luis Martinez: "A powerful first-person narrative, based on a true incident, about a sixteen-year-old boy trying to cross the Mexican/Texas border in a sweltering railroad boxcar with twelve older desperate men." (Bilingual)

Dan Wakefield recommends *Dreamtime Alice*, a memoir by Mandy Sayer: "A compelling memoir of a young woman tap-dancer who works with her musician father on streets corners of New York and New Orleans. A fine work of the memoir genre." (Ballantine)

New Books by
Our Advisory Editors

Rita Dove, *On the Bus with Rosa Parks*, poems: In her seventh collection, Dove mines American mythologies and histories to brilliant effect, arriving at relevant and artful poems that stir and sing. (Norton)

George Garrett, *Oedipus at Colonus*, play: Garrett's scintillating translation is included in *Sophocles, 2*, edited by David R. Slavitt and Palmer Bovie, which rounds out the Penn Greek Drama Series, the first complete translations of Sophocles in fifty years. (Pennsylvania)

Philip Levine, *The Mercy*, poems: Levine's eighteenth volume is at turns touching and heartbreaking, enchanting and brutal, but always compelling. This is a book of essential journeys, from birth to death, from innocence to experience, from youth to age, from here to there. (Knopf)

Robert Pinsky, *The Sounds of Poetry: A Brief Guide*, nonfiction: Going far beyond mere prosody, Pinsky delivers a fascinating, instructive treatise on poetry, which he convincingly asserts is, above all, a "vocal" and "bodily" art. (FSG)

Charles Simic, *Jackstraws*, poems: In his thirteenth collection, Simic sometimes experiments with form, but is characteristically lyrical, sly, irascible, undeniably funny. His poems continue to startle, the "big topics" mixing with everyday annoyances. (Harcourt)

CONTRIBUTOR SPOTLIGHT With her long story in this issue, Megan Staffel makes a return to our pages—indeed, to any magazine's pages—after an absence of twenty years, and this fall, her third book, *The Notebook of Lost Things,* will be published by Soho Press twelve years after her last novel saw print. It might seem that Staffel, an author of obvious talent, must have taken some sort of self-imposed hiatus from writing, but that wasn't the case. She worked doggedly in the interim, finishing two novels that she was ultimately unable to sell, and her persistence, when anyone else might have quit, is cause for marvel.

Brian Oglesbee

Megan Staffel was born in 1952 and raised in Philadelphia. Her father was a ceramic artist, her mother a painter, and Staffel intended to follow suit, enrolling in art school. Quickly, though, she changed her mind, deciding to become an actress, and transferred to Emerson College. Ironically, she never took a single acting class there, finding her true calling in a creative writing workshop. After graduating, Staffel and her husband, Graham Marks, a ceramics teacher, eventually moved to Iowa City, where she attended the Writers' Workshop, studying with Frederick Busch and Hilma Wolitzer and receiving her M.F.A. in 1980.

In 1983, James Randall, her mentor at Emerson College, published Staffel's collection of stories, *A Length of Wire,* through his small press, Pym-Randall, and in 1987, North Point released her first novel, *She Wanted Something Else.* But thereafter, she found that she couldn't get anything published. "I got sidetracked into myself, into my own history," she says. "I wrote and revised two novels for nine years, and, in retrospect, I think it's fair to say that I'm not a strong autobiographical writer. But the years of writing and not getting published were not wasted time or effort. I learned a lot about craft. I also, incidentally, figured out a lot about my life."

A few years ago, Staffel developed a very different, more sophisticated narrative voice. She polished off her new novel, *The Notebook of Lost Things*, in about a year and a half. Asked what turned it around for her, Staffel immediately answers, "I discovered fiction." She dropped the first-person viewpoint she'd always favored for third-person omniscient narration. "I was thoroughly sick of myself. That's when I discovered the power of imagining other people's lives."

She got the initial inspiration for the book playing Scrabble with one of her two children. Her son, frustrated by the game, used all of his tiles to make up a single word: ROVATYSNOTNUK. "I was just touched by the idea of someone being boxed in a corner," Staffel says, "and opting for creative means to get himself out." Thinking of such a person led directly to one of the characters in the novel, which is set in a close-knit town very much like Alfred, New York, where Staffel lives with her family (her husband switched professions and is now an acupuncturist; Staffel teaches through Vermont College's low-residency B.A. program).

"Having grown up with artists, I wasn't afraid of failure," Staffel says. "My father would lose whole kilns of work, my mother would have shows where few things sold. They never thought about quitting. It wasn't ever about success, anyway. It has to do with a private necessity. That's what keeps it all going."

FAVORITE POEMS Robert Pinsky has just finished two consecutive terms as the Poet Laureate of the United States, and he has ensured that he will be a difficult act to follow. Traditionally, the only specific duties of the poet laureate, who is appointed by the Library of Congress, are to give a lecture and reading and to introduce other writers at the Library's readings. But two years ago, Pinsky, the author of five books of poetry, most recently *The Figured Wheel*, embarked on a daunting plan for the centerpiece of his laureateship. He devised the Favorite Poem Project, recording everyday Americans reading aloud poems they love (and saying why), and then archiving two hundred videos and a thousand audio tapes of the recitations as one of the Library of Congress's millennium gifts to the nation—an end-of-the century time capsule of poems.

Pinsky's intention was to capture people from every state and every conceivable walk of life, with varying regional accents, ages, levels of education, professions, and ethnicities. Anyone could nominate a poem, as long as he or she didn't write it. Pinsky wanted to demonstrate the vigorous presence of poetry in the lives of Americans outside the insular literary world. The goal was to gather a collection not necessarily of the world's best poetry, but of the intimate bonds between Americans and the poems most meaningful to them. Pinsky has always maintained that the essential medium of poetry is the human voice. "I hope the project," he says, "will also affect the teaching of poetry—that it will foreground a personal and indeed physical relationship to a poem as an important part of the teaching of poetry."

The archive—administered by Pinsky, the New England Foundation for the Arts, the Library of Congress, and Boston University, and funded by the NEA, the Hewlett Foundation, and the Knight Foundation—will be available through a site on the World Wide Web (www.favoritepoem.org), a print anthology, and various educational products and broadcasts.

SUBSCRIBERS Please feel free to contact us by letter or e-mail with comments, address changes (the post office will not forward journals), or any problems with your subscription. Our e-mail address is: pshares@emerson.edu. Also, please note that on occasion we exchange mailing lists with other literary magazines and organizations. If you would like your name excluded from these exchanges, simply send us an e-mail message or a letter stating so.

CONTRIBUTORS' NOTES

Spring 1999

RICHARD BAKER is an artist living in New York City, where his work is represented by the Joan T. Washburn Gallery.

KAREN BRENNAN, a poet and fiction writer, won the Associated Writing Programs Award for her book of short fiction *Wild Desire.* She teaches at the University of Utah and in Warren Wilson's M.F.A. Program for Writers. "Three Seaside Tales" is from her most recent collection, *The Garden in Which I Walk.*

RAFAEL CAMPO teaches and practices general internal medicine at Harvard Medical School and Beth Israel Deaconess Medical Center in Boston. He is the author of *The Other Man Was Me* (Arté Publico, 1994), *What the Body Told* (Duke, 1996), and *The Poetry of Healing: A Doctor's Education in Empathy, Identity, and Desire* (Norton, 1996). With the support of a 1997–98 Guggenheim fellowship, he has completed work on his next collection of poems, *Diva,* which is forthcoming from Duke University Press this fall.

MICHAEL J. CARTER is a poet living in Boston.

LUCILLE CLIFTON currently serves as Distinguished Professor of Humanities at St. Mary's College of Maryland, and the Blackburn Professor of Creative Writing at Duke University. She has published ten books of poetry, most recently *Terrible Stories* (BOA, 1996; Slow Dancer, 1998). Her most recent awards include a 1999–2002 Lila Wallace–Reader's Digest Fund Artist Award and a 1997 Lannan Foundation Achievement Award in Poetry. In 1998 she was inducted into Phi Beta Kappa and the National Literature Hall of Fame for African American Writers.

BERNARD COOPER's most recent book is *Truth Serum.* His work has appeared in *The Best American Essays, Prize Stories: The O. Henry Awards, Harper's,* and *Story.* "Hunters and Gatherers" is from *Guess Again,* a collection of short fiction forthcoming from Simon & Schuster.

ALICE FULTON's most recent book of poems is *Sensual Math* (Norton). Her collection of essays, *Feeling as a Foreign Language: The Good Strangeness of Poetry,* has just been published by Graywolf Press. She is currently Professor of English at the University of Michigan, Ann Arbor.

AMY GERSTLER is a writer of poetry, prose, and journalism. A book of her poems, *Medicine,* is scheduled to be published in 2000 by Penguin Putman. Her two most recent books are *Nerve Storm* and *Crown of Weeds.*

JUDITH GROSSMAN is a fiction writer and critic who grew up in England and now commutes between Maryland and Massachusetts. "How Aliens Think" is the title story of a collection to be published by Johns Hopkins University Press. She is also the author of a novel, *Her Own Terms* (Soho).

MARILYN HACKER is the author of nine books, including *Presentation Piece,* which received the National Book Award in 1975, *Winter Numbers,* which received a Lambda Literary Award and the Lenore Marshall Award, both in 1995, and the verse novel *Love, Death, and the Changing of the Seasons.* In 1996, Wake Forest University Press published *Edge,* her translations of the French poet Claire Malroux, and her *Selected Poems* was awarded the Poets' Prize. Her new book, *Squares and Courtyards,* will be published by W.W. Norton this fall.

FORREST HAMER's first book of poems, *Call & Response* (Alice James, 1995), won the Beatrice Hawley Award, and has gone into a second printing.

BOB HICOK's *Plus Shipping* is just out from BOA Editions. *The Legend of Light* (Wisconsin, 1995) won the Felix Pollak Prize and was an ALA Booklist Notable Book of the Year. An NEA fellow this year, he will also have a poem in *The Best American Poetry 1999.*

SCOTT HIGHTOWER is originally from Texas and now teaches at NYU/Gallatin. His poems have appeared in a number of publications. He is a contributing editor to *The Journal.*

BRENDA HILLMAN is the author of two chapbooks, *Coffee, Three A.M.* and *Autumn Sojourn,* and of five collections of poetry, the most recent of which are *Bright Existence* and *Loose Sugar.* She teaches at St. Mary's College in Moraga, California.

TONY HOAGLAND's first collection of poems, *Sweet Ruin* (Wisconsin), won the Brittingham Prize in Poetry and the John C. Zacharis First Book Award from *Ploughshares.* His second collection, *Donkey Gospel* (Graywolf), won the James Laughlin Award from the Academy of American Poets. His poem "Lawrence," which first appeared in *Ploughshares,* was chosen by Robert Bly for *The Best American Poetry 1999.*

GRAY JACOBIK was the 1998 winner of the X. J. Kennedy Poetry Prize. Her new book, *The Surface of Last Scattering,* is just out from Texas Review Press. *The Double Task* received the 1997 Juniper Prize, and was published by University of Massachusetts Press. Recent poems appear in *The Kenyon Review, Ontario Review, LUNA,* and *Sycamore Review.*

ANTONIO JOCSON received his M.F.A. from the University of Iowa Writers' Workshop. He has published six books for children and several sailing guides. His poetry has appeared in various anthologies and literary journals. He lives in Houston and Manila, Philippines.

KATE KNAPP JOHNSON is the author of two collections of poetry, *When Orchids Were Flowers* (Dragon Gate) and *This Perfect Life* (Miami Univ.). She teaches at Sarah Lawrence College's writing program and lives in Mt. Kisco, New York, with her husband and children.

CAROLYN KIZER founded *Poetry Northwest* in 1959 with Richard Hugo, and she was the first Director of Literary Programs at the NEA. Subsequently, she has taught and read at many universities, including North Carolina, Columbia, Princeton, and Stanford. She won the Pulitzer Prize in 1985 for *YIN: New Poems*. Her latest books are *100 Great Poems by Women*, which she edited for Ecco Press, and *Harping On: Poems 1985–1995* (Copper Canyon).

WAYNE KOESTENBAUM's third book of poetry, *The Milk of Inquiry*, will be published this spring by Persea. He is a professor of English at the Graduate School of the City University of New York.

DANA LEVIN's first book, *In the Surgical Theatre*, was chosen by Louise Glück for *The American Poetry Review*/Honickman First Book Prize, and will be published by Copper Canyon this fall. She is a 1999 recipient of a literary fellowship from the NEA.

CYNTHIA MACDONALD is the author of six collections of poetry, most recently *I Can't Remember* (Knopf). She is a professor at the University of Houston, where she founded the creative writing program in 1979.

KATHRYN MARIS's work appeared most recently in *Columbia Magazine*. She lives in London, where she is completing her first book of poems.

JACK MARTIN received his M.F.A. from Colorado State University. His poems have appeared in *ACM, Agni, Black Warrior Review, Dry Creek Review, Fine Madness, The Journal, River Styx*, and other magazines. His chapbook is *Weekend Sentences* (Pudding House, 1997). He lives in Fort Collins, Colorado, with his wife and son.

GAIL MAZUR is the author of three books of poems, *Nightfire, The Pose of Happiness*, and *The Common* (Chicago, 1995), and has recently completed a fourth, *They Can't Take That Away from Me*. She lives in Cambridge, Massachusetts, where she is the founding director of the Blacksmith House Poetry Reading Series. She has been Poet-in-Residence in Emerson College's M.F.A. Program in Writing, Literature, and Publishing since 1996, and also teaches in the Fine Arts Work Center in Provincetown's summer program.

SANDRA MCPHERSON's two collections, *Edge Effect* and *The Spaces Between Birds*, were published simultaneously by Wesleyan in 1996. Janus Press handprinted *Beauty in Use*, poems and paper quilts, in 1997. Besides teaching at the University of California at Davis, she sells antiques under the name *allmyquilts* on eBay on the Internet.

JEREDITH MERRIN is Professor of English at the Ohio State University and is the author of *An Enabling Humility: Marianne Moore, Elizabeth Bishop, and the Uses of Tradition*. Her first collection of poems, *Shift*, was published by the University of Chicago Press in 1996.

SUSAN MITCHELL's most recent book of poems, *Rapture*, won the first Kingsley Tufts Award and was a National Book Award finalist. She has received grants from the Guggenheim and Lannan foundations. Her third book, *Erotikon,* is forthcoming from HarperCollins. She teaches in the graduate creative writing program at Florida Atlantic University.

CAROL MUSKE (Carol Muske Dukes in fiction) teaches creative writing at the University of Southern California. Her most recent books are *An Octave Above Thunder* (Penguin, 1997) and *Women and Poetry* (Michigan, 1997). She is a 1997 Witter Bynner fellow (Library of Congress), and was a recipient of two Pushcart Prizes in 1998.

SHARON OLDS teaches at New York University. *Blood, Tin, Straw* will be published by Knopf in September 1999. She is New York State Poet Laureate for 1998–2000.

JULIE PAEGLE is an M.F.A. student and writing instructor at the University of Utah. She divides her time between Salt Lake City, southern Utah, and her cabin in Murphy Dome, Alaska. This is her first published poem.

RICARDO PAU-LLOSA's last two books of poetry, *Cuba* and *Vereda Tropical,* were published by Carnegie-Mellon University Press. His most recent books on art are *Rafael Soriano and the Poetics of Light* and a forthcoming monograph on the Puerto Rican painter Julio Rosado del Valle.

ROBERT PINSKY has just finished serving two terms as Poet Laureate of the United States. His most recent books are *The Sounds of Poetry: A Brief Guide* (FSG, 1998) and *The Handbook of Heartbreak,* an anthology (Morrow, 1998). He teaches in the graduate writing program at Boston University.

JAMES RICHARDSON's *How Things Are* will be published by Carnegie-Mellon University Press in 2000. He has poems and aphorisms in recent issues of *The Yale Review, Ontario Review, The Georgia Review,* and *Michigan Quarterly Review.* He teaches at Princeton University.

REGINALD SHEPHERD's third book, *Wrong,* is due from University of Pittsburgh Press this fall. Pittsburgh also published his two previous books, *Some Are Drowning,* which won an AWP Award in 1993, and *Angel, Interrupted.* A recipient of fellowships from the NEA and the Illinois Arts Council, he lives in Chicago.

MEGAN STAFFEL has published a novel and a collection of stories. Her second novel, *The Notebook of Lost Things,* is forthcoming from Soho Press in August 1999. She lives with her family in western New York State and teaches at Vermont College. See page 197 for a "Contributor Spotlight" profile on Staffel.

LYNN STANLEY earned her B.A. from Smith College in 1997 and is currently working toward her M.F.A. at the University of Michigan. She is the editor/publisher of the Naked Poet Press, which specializes in handmade books and broadsides. She lives in Ann Arbor and Truro, Massachusetts. "The Gift" will appear in *Gravity Claims Us,* a chapbook from Folly Cove Books.

MYRNA STONE's poems have appeared in *Poetry, TriQuarterly, Boston Review,* and, most recently, *Green Mountains Review.* She is a current recipient of a full fellowship from Vermont Studio Center, and has just been awarded her second fellowship from the Ohio Arts Council. Her first collection, *The Art of Loss,* will be issued by Michigan State University Press in 2000.

VIRGINIA CHASE SUTTON's poems have appeared in *The Paris Review, The Antioch Review, Boulevard, Quarterly West,* and other publications. Her poetry manuscript, *Netting the Gaudy Pearls,* has been a finalist for the Walt Whitman Award, the National Poetry Series, and many other competitions. She teaches writing and lives in Phoenix, Arizona.

JENNIFER TONGE holds an M.F.A. from the University of Utah. She is a past recipient of the Wisconsin Institute for Creative Writing's Jay C. and Ruth Halls Poetry Fellowship and of a Bread Loaf Writers' Conference Work-Study Scholarship. Her poems have appeared recently in *New England Review* and *Poetry.* She lives in Salt Lake City.

REETIKA VAZIRANI is Margaret Banister Writer-in-Residence at Sweet Briar College and author of *White Elephants* (Beacon, 1996). She is a graduate of Wellesley College and the University of Virginia. Poems from two new manuscripts will appear in *The Paris Review, Western Humanities Review, Agni,* and *The American Voice Anthology of Poetry.* She is a recipient of a 1998 *Poets & Writers* Exchange Program Award.

JONAH WINTER writes and illustrates children's books for a living. His most recent book, *Fair Ball! 14 Great Stars from Baseball's Negro Leagues,* is available in bookstores.

DAVID WOJAHN's most recent collection, *The Falling Hour,* appeared from the University of Pittsburgh Press in 1997. He teaches at Indiana University, and, for the 1998–99 academic year, he is Sherry Visiting Professor of Poetry at the University of Chicago.

SUSAN WOOD is a Guggenheim fellow this year and is completing a new volume of poems. Her *Campo Santo* was the Lamont selection in 1991. She teaches at Rice University.

∾

HOW IT WORKS *Ploughshares* is published three times a year: mixed issues of poetry and fiction in the Spring and Winter and a fiction issue in the Fall, with each guest-edited by a different writer of prominence, usually one whose early work was published in the journal. Guest editors are invited to solicit up to half of their issues, with the other half selected from unsolicited manuscripts screened for them by staff editors. This guest-editor policy is designed to introduce readers to different literary circles and tastes, and to offer a fuller representation of the range and diversity of contemporary letters than would be possible with a single editorship. Yet, at the same time, we expect every issue to reflect our overall standards of literary excellence. We liken *Ploughshares* to a theater company: each issue might have a different guest editor and different writers—just as a play will have a different director, playwright, and cast—but subscribers can count on a governing aesthetic, a consistency in literary values and quality, that is uniquely our own.

SUBMISSION POLICIES We welcome unsolicited manuscripts from August 1 to March 31 (postmark dates). All submissions sent from April to July are returned unread. In the past, guest editors often announced specific themes for issues, but we have revised our editorial policies and no longer restrict submissions to thematic topics. Submit your work at any time during our reading period; if a manuscript is not timely for one issue, it will be considered for another. We do not recommend trying to target specific guest editors. Our backlog is unpredictable, and staff editors ultimately have the responsibility of determining for which editor a work is most appropriate. Mail one prose piece and/or one to three poems at a time (mail genres separately). No e-mail submissions. Poems should be individually typed either single- or double-spaced on one side of the page. Prose should be typed double-spaced on one side and be no longer than twenty-five pages. Although we look primarily for short stories, we occasionally publish personal essays/memoirs. Novel excerpts are acceptable if self-contained. Unsolicited book reviews and criticism are not considered. Please do not send multiple submissions of the same genre, and do not send another manuscript until you hear about the first. *No more than a total of two submissions per reading period.* Additional submissions will be returned unread. Mail your manuscript in a page-size manila envelope, your full name and address written on the outside. In general, address submissions to the "Fiction Editor," "Poetry Editor," or "Nonfiction Editor," not to the guest or staff editors by name, unless you have a legitimate association with them or have been previously published in the magazine. Unsolicited work sent directly to a guest editor's home or office will be ignored and discarded; guest editors are formally instructed not to read such work. All manuscripts and correspondence regarding submissions should be accompanied by a self-addressed, stamped envelope (s.a.s.e.) for a response; no replies will be given by e-mail or postcard. Expect three to five months for a decision. We now receive over a thousand manuscripts a month. Do not query us until five months have passed, and if you do, please write to us, including an s.a.s.e. and indicating the postmark date of submission, instead of calling or e-mailing. Simultaneous submissions are amenable as long as they are indicated as such and we are notified immediately upon acceptance elsewhere. We cannot accommodate revisions, changes of return address, or forgotten s.a.s.e.'s after the fact. We do not reprint previously published work. Translations are welcome if permission has been granted. We cannot be responsible for delay, loss, or damage. Payment is upon publication: $25/printed page, $50 minimum per title, $250 maximum per author, with two copies of the issue and a one-year subscription. These rates are for 1999 only. Because of the loss of major funding, rates will be lower in 2000.

Ploughshares
Patrons

This nonprofit publication would not be possible without the support of our readers and the generosity of the following individuals and organizations.

COUNCIL: $3,000 for two lifetime subscriptions, acknowledgement in the journal for three years, and votes on the Cohen and Zacharis Awards.
PATRON: $1,000 for a lifetime subscription and acknowledgement in the journal for two years.
FRIEND: $500 for a lifetime subscription and acknowledgement in the journal for one year.
All donations are tax-deductible.
Please make your check payable to
Ploughshares, Emerson College,
100 Beacon St., Boston, MA 02116.

Marion Ettlinger

IN MEMORIAM
ANDRE DUBUS
1936–1999

The Lieutenant
Separate Flights
Adultery & Other Choices
Finding a Girl in America
The Times Are Never So Bad
Voices from the Moon
The Last Worthless Evening
Selected Stories
Broken Vessels
Dancing After Hours
Meditations from a Movable Chair

BENNINGTON WRITING SEMINARS

MFA in Writing and Literature
Two-Year Low-Residency Program

A. BLAKE GARDNER

FICTION
NONFICTION
POETRY

Jane Kenyon Poetry Scholarships available
For more information contact:
Writing Seminars
Box PL
Bennington College
Bennington, VT 05201
802-440-4452, Fax 802-447-4269

Graywolf Forum 3: The Business of Memory:

The Art of Remembering in an Age of Forgetting

Edited by CHARLES BAXTER

Baxter invited Richard Bausch, Margot Livesey, James Alan McPherson, and other creative writers to reflect on memoir, memory, and forgetfulness. The resulting essays address a provocative range of topics: the explosion of interest in the memoir, the recovered-memory movement, America in the grip of an "amnesia plague," and the need for coherent stories of our past to help us organize our present.

Paperback, $16.00 (1-55597-287-X) Available in May

Tug

G.E. PATTERSON

"In the poem 'Yard Talk,' G.E. Patterson writes of the 'hard love' black men express between each other, but the true conversation in the poem and in this stunning debut is with all of us. You will have to travel far to find a book that tackles the interior landscape of a black man with such tenderness and lyric power. *Tug* is the book I know had to come down the pike sooner or later. Reading it, I couldn't ignore the feeling that a fire was being lit under American poetry." *Cornelius Eady*

Paperback, $12.95 (1-55597-285-3)

The Wedding Jester

STEVE STERN

"To be a true inheritor of a tradition carries with it the responsibility of expanding that tradition and keeping it vital. In *The Wedding Jester,* Steve Stern does both. Only a writer with a deep reverence for and a connection with the ancient story-telling power of his rich folkloric sources could concoct the often irreverently comic twists that distinguish these genuinely marvelous—and always vital—stories." *Stuart Dybek*

Paperback, $14.00 (1-55597-290-X)

The Way It Is: *New and Selected Poems*

WILLIAM STAFFORD

"Stafford, a National Book Award winner and once Oregon's Poet Laureate, left behind a body of work that represents some of the finest poetry written during the second half of this century. . . . The poems, which reveal many of Stafford's themes—his affinity for Native Americans, love of nature, protest of war, and concern about the dangers of technology—are subtle and powerful in tone, but imagery is paramount. . . . Highly recommended." *Library Journal*

Available in Paperback, $16.00 (1-55597-284-5)

A RARE BREED OF PUBLISHER FOR 25 YEARS

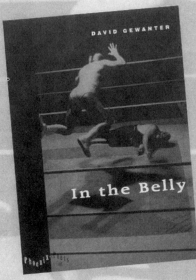

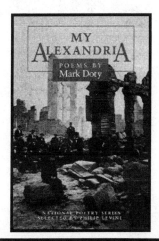

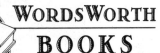

the modern writer as witness

Special Issue
American Families

Volume XII Number 2 $7   1998

Contributors

Marcia Aldrich
Pete Fromm
Dan Gerber
Jean Ross Justice
Julia Kasdorf
Anna Keesey
Maxine Kumin
Thomas Lynch
Joseph McElroy
Roland Merullo
Kent Nelson
Linda Pastan
Maureen Seaton
Floyd Skloot
Paul West

"*From its inception, the vision that distinguishes* Witness *has been consistent: it is a magazine situated at the intersection of ideas and passions, a magazine energized by the intellect, yet one in which thought is never presented as abstraction, but rather as life blood. Each issue is beautifully produced and eminently readable.*"

Stuart Dybek

Call for Manuscripts:

Witness invites submission of memoirs, essays, fiction, poetry and artwork for a special 1999 issue on **Love in America.**
Deadline: July 15, 1999.

Writings from *Witness* have been selected for inclusion in *Best American Essays, Best American Poetry, Prize Stories: The O. Henry Awards,* and *The Pushcart Prizes.*